DR. GARY GOODMAN

TELEMARKETING FOR
NON-TELEMARKETERS

ILLUSTRATIONS: RANDALL ENOS

Dartnell is a publisher serving the world of business with books, manuals, newsletters, and training materials for executives, managers, supervisors, salespeople, financial officials, personnel executives, and office employees. Dartnell also produces management and sales training videos and audiocassettes, and publishes many useful business forms, and many of its materials and films are available in languages other than English. Dartnell, established in 1917, serves the world's business community. For details, catalogs, and product information, write to:

THE DARTNELL CORPORATION
4660 N Ravenswood Ave
Chicago, IL 60640-4595, U.S.A.
Or phone (800) 621-5463 in U.S. and Canada
www.dartnellcorp.com

CONTENTS

DEDICATION

To my wife, best friend, and colleague,

Dr. Deanne Goodman,

and to our daughter, the wonderful

Amanda Leigh

ACKNOWLEDGMENTS

I would like to thank Jessica Wainwright, my agent from the Literary Group International, and Scott Pemberton, my editor at Dartnell, for their support and encouragement in developing this book.

I would also like to express my appreciation to my consulting clients, as well as to you, the reader.

CHAPTER ONE

WHY PEOPLE LOVE TO HATE TELEMARKETING
AND WHAT WE CAN DO ABOUT IT

If you want to create a minor ruckus, just go to a party or to a backyard barbecue and tell people that you're a telemarketer. You're likely to hear at least one person say:

> *"You're not one of those people who call us at home, are you? How can you do that?"*

So why would any decent person, like you, want to read a book about telemarketing? In a word, because telemarketing is a necessary endeavor. If you do anything in the world of business or the professions or even in the nonprofit sector, being telephonically effective will give you a distinct advantage.

There are ways to make telemarketing not only effective from a commercial standpoint but also enjoyable for sellers as well as for buyers. It can be a very rewarding medium of communication and commerce.

The days in which people could linger over leisurely face-to-face conversations are coming to an end. Today people expect to do business at satellite speed. If we're going to have meaningful conversations and sell things efficiently, salespeople will need to become proficient at influencing and persuading from afar. That's where the phone comes in.

The phone is an instantaneous, highly interpersonal, and inexpensive medium. And now that we're experiencing waves of deregulation, telecommunicating is getting cheaper every year. A long-distance call that cost a dollar about five years ago can now be completed for about a tenth of that price.

But no one is *born* telephonically effective. Telephone skills must be learned. I've been teaching telephone techniques and telephone sales for about 20 years. Selling by phone put me through college, and this capability enabled me to start a very successful, nationwide consulting practice — without financial backing.

I've also written a number of best-sellers, including *Reach Out & Sell Someone* and *You Can Sell Anything By Telephone!* But these books are written primarily for people who *want* to be telemarketers.

This book is designed for people who may not like telemarketing as it is widely practiced. This book intends to help people who need to get more done in less time and who need to make sales or engineer consent smoothly. This book is also for folks who, if they must persuade, need to do so on a soft-sell, friendly basis, without coming across to others (or to themselves) as telemarketers.

I have good news for you. You can be a normal, healthy, well-balanced, even nice person, *and* succeed in telemarketing. But you are going to need the special techniques that I provide in this book to make the most of your personality strengths.

I refer to the sum total of these techniques as *The New, Polite Telemarketing*™. Throughout this book I point out how the methods I'm demonstrating are innovative and state of the art, as well as congenial. You'll also see how they're completely honest, professional, and tremendously successful.

It's not my goal to turn you into an instant super-salesperson, though I'd love to hear that you reach this stature. I assume you're already a super person. My job is to help you to stay that way as you develop new telephone skills. You shouldn't have to sell your soul simply to develop additional capabilities. If you had to, it wouldn't be a fair bargain, would it?

Why Telemarketing Has Earned a Bad Reputation

There's nothing inherently wrong with using the telephone, whether for social or for business purposes. But *how* we use it can make all the difference in the productivity it offers, and how we and others feel about our transactions.

Telemarketing has earned a mixed report card in recent years. On the one hand, it has helped business people and professionals to cut down on travel expenses and to communicate with more people in less time. But it has failed in many ways while offending millions of people. Before charting a better course in this book, we need to examine how "traditional" telemarketing has run aground.

Why do some people love to hate telemarketing even more than they despise "junk mail" and obnoxious radio and television ads? I've been a guest on scores of radio and TV shows, and callers say they're peeved about a number of things:

- Some consumers dislike the idea of being called at home, for any purpose. They consider it an invasion of their privacy.

- Some dislike being disturbed while they're involved in other activities that require concentration.

- Many say that telemarketers sound "phony," as if they're reading from scripts, so consumers become distrustful about buying over the phone.

- Others are afraid of being victimized by "tele-scams," in which consumers have been defrauded by unscrupulous callers.

- Increasing numbers of intelligent recipients of calls find telemarketing strategies "dumb." They cite a classic example of sellers who try to vend aluminum siding to folks who own brick homes.

These concerns are valid and important, but I don't think they quite capture the most significant reason people are peeved with this medium: I believe the great majority of people are upset with the adversarial, "us-against-them" way they've been communicated with after calls have begun.

Traditional telemarketing has *never* been popular among those who are called. It is like a boxer who clings to the ropes and gets bloodied throughout an entire bout but in the final round miraculously triumphs. This medium is an unlikely survivor in an atmosphere of widespread customer resentment.

Frankly, other sales media are a heck of a lot easier to use. Direct mail employs paper, postage, and persuasive copy, with few nasty interchanges between buyers and sellers. Display advertising and the Internet work in much the same way. They're almost antiseptic in their approaches to attracting and serving customers.

For decades, some telemarketing firms have used a scorched-earth policy in how they treat customers. Acting as if there is no tomorrow, these salespeople "sprayed-and-prayed" through billions of one-sided, manipulative, and often-shady sales talks.

Customers have been lied to, oversold, sworn at, and otherwise degraded. They've been phoned late in the evening and on Sundays. Conversations have been illegally bugged and tape recorded, violating privacy rights.

Some of these practices have been dramatized in movies such as *Tin Men* and *Glengarry Glen Ross*.

And life hasn't been rosy for those who labor on the phones. Telemarketers often subsist on depressed wages, given the difficulty of their tasks. And they frequently encounter angry prospects.

Being hung-up on, say fifty or even a hundred times a day, five days a week, isn't a picnic. Rejection can exact a toll on the psyches of phone people and the purses of their employers.

Commonly, companies that telemarket experience 100 percent employee turnover each three months — or 400 percent per year. I've consulted to firms that experience 1,200 percent annual turnover.

At an estimated cost of up to $5,000, to recruit, hire, train, supervise, and lose a person after three months, this expense adds up to billions of dollars of lost productivity annually.

In light of such negative circumstances, why hasn't this punchy fighter we know as traditional telemarketing gone down for the count and stayed down? Why does it keep bouncing back and, in the main, keep prospering?

There are some important reasons. One of them is explained by analogy. A few decades ago, Paul Erlich wrote a book called *The Population Bomb*, in which he used then-current statistics regarding population growth and the food supply. He predicted we would now be living in a world of widespread famines and political revolutions.

But are we? Certainly, some areas of the world have severe problems but not nearly on the scale that Erlich predicted. What he didn't take into account can be captured in a single word: *technology*.

There has been a technological revolution in agriculture that has increased the yield from planting. So there is more food, and despite the fact that there have been surges in the population, many new mouths are being fed.

Traditional telemarketing methods have bred resentment among consumers, so more of them have become resistant to buying. A few years ago, the economics of making calls looked pretty negative. As customers grew more hostile, it took more and more calls for tellsellers to get positive results.

But then new technologies came to the rescue in the form of software and automatic dialers that could multiply the number of sales pitches telemarketers completed in a day of calling.

Telemarketing companies that now use such technology have gone public through stock offerings and are being embraced by investors and by Wall Street. Telemarketing is helping companies both to downsize expensive field sales forces and to outsource at the same time. It is a part of the "creative destruction" cycle that economists say is inevitable, whereby more expensive processes are supplanted by cheaper ones. So, in a sense, these are the best of times *and* the worst of times for telemarketing.

And the fundamental flaw of telemarketing — its adversarial communication style — can be masked, at least temporarily, by the new economies of making calls. In other words, so what if calls are poor in communication quality? Companies can make so many calls at such a low cost that it doesn't matter!

This kind of thinking simply can't last. It's akin to saying, "So what if fluorocarbons are blowing holes in the ozone layer the size of Australia? We'll simply invent better sunscreens!"

An ecological principle should inform how we do our telemarketing.

Just as strip-mining is devastating to the countryside, if the land isn't restored, people who work the phones should actively promote the regeneration of goodwill among those called. Telemarketers should focus not only on making sales but on establishing harmony in customer relations. And it's achievable, they can do it!

Numerous newspaper circulation sales managers report that hordes of consumers are demanding to be placed on "do not call" lists. This is diminishing the calling-base of the publications, and if the trend persists, newspapers will literally call their way out of the newspaper business.

It's an ecological disaster as real as overfishing or overplanting of land. Many firms in other industries that do heavy telemarketing are facing the same decline in their customer-calling base.

The solution is clear: We need a New, Polite Telemarketing — one that is so effective that nontelemarketers can succeed with it. Am I suggesting that we simply start sounding nicer?

That would be a good place to begin, but by a Polite Telemarketing I mean one that dramatically improves the quality of our communication techniques and the impacts that they have on our customers, communities, and us.

A better telemarketing system should meet these requirements:

- It needs to feel comfortable for buyers and sellers.
- It needs to reduce telemarketing representative turnover and contribute to industry stability.
- It needs to attract, instead of repel, capable, wholesome people.
- It needs to make it easier to sell instead of making it progressively more difficult.
- It needs to discourage hostile legislation.
- It needs to reduce the negative image that the occupation and industry bear today.
- It needs to reduce job stress so telemarketers can work full-time shifts, if they prefer, without wear-and-tear.
- It needs to build on positive communication practices.
- It needs to be more economically efficient than the telemarketing styles it replaces.

In a word, it needs to be the kind of telemarketing that your Mom could feel good about!

Traditional Telemarketing: "It's Just Not *Me*!"

I didn't arrive at the concept of enhancing telemarketing overnight. I've been a phone rep, a manager, and a consultant. My consulting clients have included the best and the brightest telemarketing firms, and I've done well for them, and with them. But it always bothered me that we seemed to fail much more than we succeeded in building stable teleselling organizations and enduring customer bases.

And then, when I was staffing my own in-house telemarketing function, the lesson really hit home for me. I hired a waitress to make outbound calls. Having years of experience in telemarketing management and consulting, I thought I had spotted a winner. She made sales for me instantly, and within a week, she doubled what she was earning at the restaurant.

But by the second week, she began to wear a long face. Then, she said she wanted to speak to me. Walking into my office, she declared with a weary, burned-out tone, "I just can't do it anymore."

"How come?" I asked, dumbfounded.

"Well, you see, it's just not *me*."

I'm normally not at a loss for words, but this was an exceptional situation. As a pro, I'm not used to losing people so quickly.

She couldn't sell the way I wanted her to sell and still feel good about herself and her job. *Her personal identity was at war with the traditional telemarketing process.*

That event prompted me to rethink my assumptions about traditional telemarketing. I saw that we were losing people who would stay if we offered them another selling style. One that was a better fit for their personalities. One that was more conversational, friendly, easygoing, and pressure-free. One that nontelemarketers could embrace.

I felt driven to invent this new approach. What I came up with has been praised as nothing less than a breakthrough. It not only works with novices but also doubles the results of experienced professionals.

This new method has proven its value to hundreds of companies and to thousands of individuals. It has been a successful on-site program as well as a popular national seminar. I also developed an acclaimed five-hour, 10-cassette, studio-taped version of the program, with a 63-page learning guide.

Reactions to this information have been extremely positive:

Target Marketing magazine says the techniques represent "a new school of thought" about telemarketing that "encourages customer interaction, promotes effective time management by TSRs (telemarketing sales representatives) and helps eliminate TSR turnover due to the wear-and-tear of selling by phone."

TeleProfessional magazine says the techniques are "great" and that these methods are "not mere speculation, but tested and proven techniques to improve the quality of telemarketing calls while garnering more sales."

The Distributor's & Wholesaler's Advisor reports that this New Telemarketing is "very humanistic when compared to the 'old style' of telemarketing, which put customers on the spot."

Ruth Jack, who sells for Advanced Promotions, says: "Gary's tapes have doubled our sales!" Jim Martini, who sells for Siemens, says: "Because of your techniques I haven't missed yet in getting through secretaries and screens!"

Tyler Martin, who sells for ShareData, says: "The T-Funnel method for asking questions is really innovative and helpful." Suzanne Bell, who manages for Airco Gas & Gear, says: "Your ideas are fantastic. They really pump us up and everyone enjoys them!"

One of the reactions that we prize the most comes from a true authority in continuing education: David Hicks, president of Success Motivation Institute. He says this program "will help anyone!"

This book aims to help you to:

- **Glide through secretarial screening and voice mail.**
  If you do business-to-business calling, you'll sell a lot more if the screener puts you through to the decision maker. This book shows you how to get through twice as often by being polite and professional.

- **Prepare for phone work.** You'll master the logistical and psychological challenges of selling by phone.

- **Avoid the pitfalls of traditional telemarketing while utilizing its strengths.** The old approach to telemarketing fails miserably in relationship selling, but it can be a tool of choice in certain simple transactions.

- **Set solid field sales appointments as well as "telephone" appointments.** Eliminate the weasel words that are ruining your appointment-setting efforts. Hear proven language for setting appointments that will get the attention and commitment of buyers.

- **Handle the toughest objections while controlling conversations.** What are the diplomatic ways that we can address objections? Which objections should we be persuaded by? How can Polite Telemarketing prevent objections, rejection, and conflict? You'll learn methods for politely avoiding objections.

- **Build your credibility with your first sentence.** Learn what a "credibility statement" is and how it is the key ingredient millionaire-salespeople use to get the attention of powerful and cynical buyers.

- **Stay positive toward telephone work.** What can you tell yourself that will keep you psyched-up about the next call? You'll learn several ways to stay positive toward telemarketing.

- **Put the power of a new, Polite Telemarketing to work.** Learn how Polite Telemarketing not only feels better for all parties but also has achieved sales where the old telemarketing failed. You'll learn the key differences between the old style and the new.

- **Learn to ask Perfect Questions.** Psychology tells us that we don't persuade other people nearly as much as they choose to persuade themselves. This book provides examples of questions that have been proven to encourage customers to buy immediately while feeling good about the entire transaction.

You'll learn all these things, and more, in the pages that follow.

Now, it's time to get down to business and to show you exactly how to become a consummate telephone professional.

Chapter Two shows you how to make the best first impression you can as you start your calls.

CHAPTER TWO

THE POLITE AND PROFESSIONAL WAY TO BEGIN YOUR CALLS

It has been said time and again that "Well begun is half done." If we can only start off on the right foot with people and make a good first impression, we're on our way to succeeding.

But the sad fact is that most telemarketing calls begin very poorly, and this is a major reason they fail. They're flawed in a number of ways. This chapter will point out these shortcomings while providing a systematic, step-by-step set of pointers for getting calls underway, the polite, professional, and successful way.

INSTRUCTION 1
SLOW DOWN AT THE BEGINNING

As a rule, telemarketers don't allow the listener to really *hear* and to *process* who is calling and for what purpose. This frustrates prospects, who make negative snap judgments about callers.

Why are telemarketers such jackrabbits as calls begin? The salespeople are afraid they'll be rejected if they proceed slowly. But they're deluding themselves, and they end up evoking the rejection that they fear.

Self-confident people, by comparison, don't fear rejection. They take their time in expressing themselves at the beginning of conversations. They recognize that listeners need a chance to assimilate what they're hearing, and a chance to buy into the purpose of the call.

Con artists intentionally speak too swiftly to be comprehended. These flim-flam folks don't want people to really hear who they are or the names of their businesses. They don't want to be tracked down later.

Amateurs also figure that the mundane details they share as a call begins aren't really important, and that they're secondary to the persuasive impact of the call. But they're dead wrong.

Style *is* content at the beginning of a call. If you rush, you induce the prospect to emulate you and to rush to judgment in determining that he or she is not interested in what you have to say or in what you're selling. Speed causes rejections.

Communicators who rush suffer from what I call "seller's mouth," and listeners interpret this signal as a chance to cut losses and to duck the major part of the call. So they defend themselves by striking out with an objection: "Sorry, not interested."

We interpret these quickie rejections to mean that people simply don't like telemarketing calls. Some don't, but super-early rejection in a call is really a bad report card for how the telemarketer performed in that part of the encounter.

Some phone people will ask, "But if I slow down, won't I *invite* interruptions?" Occasionally this happens, but you'll avoid a lot more, because you'll seem to know what you're doing. You'll sound as though you have something important to say, and most folks will be less inclined to cut you off if they get this impression.

How slowly should you speak at the beginning? Let me put it into perspective. The average speaker utters 100 – 150 words per minute. Slow down to about 60 – 75 words per minute in your first sentence or two on the phone.

At first, this will seem painfully slow to you. Don't worry about that. You want to send a signal of confidence to the listener, and taking your time will help.

Instruction 2:
Ask the Person's Name — Don't State it

Imagine calling Bill Smith. You may already know his name, so the tendency is to state his name with a flat, matter-of-fact tone: "Hello, Bill, this is Gary Goodman ..."

I have a better way.

Say, "Hello, Bill?" Then wait for him to respond. After he replies, continue with, "This is so-and-so ..."

What's the difference? It's major. By *asking* his name, you make sure it's Bill and not someone else. More important is that when you ask his name, he'll elevate his voice, as well as his emotional level when he responds.

"Yes!" is how he'll react, instead of "Uh-huh." Without his knowing it, you'll make him sound optimistic about what is to follow in the call, whereas if you declared the prospect's name, he'd sound bored and negative.

It's a heck of a lot easier to communicate with or to sell an optimistic, upbeat voice than a negative one, believe me! There is another interesting dimension to this strategy.

With the question you'll literally set the tone for the conversation and you'll establish a pattern of encouraging the listener to react to your agenda, instead of reacting, passively, to his. When you progress to later portions of the conversation he'll be more likely to follow your lead as a consequence of what you've done so simply in the first few seconds.

INSTRUCTION 3:
MENTION YOUR COMPANY NAME AND FOLLOW IT
WITH A CREDIBILITY STATEMENT

Recently, Bell Laboratories, the brilliant former division of AT&T, changed its name to Lucent Technologies. Bell Labs, as it was known, brought us the first transistor and the first video phone, to name a few of its products.

The Bell name, based on the old Bell System, was world renowned. So, if you had called a firm and you said you were with Bell Labs, a division of AT&T, you'd have all the credibility you needed.

As of this writing, the new name isn't nearly as well recognized. Nor are most company names to most prospects. So, consider how foolish it is to start a presentation and to say:

> Hello, Mr. Smith? This is Gary Goodman with Lucent Technologies. How are you? Good. The reason I'm calling is to introduce a new product that we've developed for the printing industry.

What's wrong with this opening? It doesn't explain who or what Lucent is. The crucial element that's missing is what I call a *credibility statement*. This is a short phrase that assigns status and clout to your firm's name so that listeners will be impressed enough to allow you to continue with your presentation.

I'd probably revise the introduction in this way:

> Hello, Mr. Smith? This is Gary Goodman with Lucent Technologies. We used to be known as AT&T's Bell Laboratories. How are you? Good. The reason I'm calling is to introduce a new product that we've developed for the printing industry.

That's pretty simple, isn't it? The wording helps because it decodes the mystery about what Lucent is, which is something that could easily vex the listener.

Here's another example:

> Hello, Ms. Jones? I'm Gary Goodman, editor of the "Sales & Service Newsletter." You may know me from my best-selling books, *Selling Skills for the Non-Salesperson* and *You Can Sell Anything by Telephone!* How are you? Good. The reason I'm calling is …

One of my consulting clients sells bond funds to investment officers at colleges. The company's salespeople used to get on the phone and mention their names and just start explaining their services.

I had them insert a credibility statement that made them a lot more money. It said, "We work with a number of colleges and universities in Texas." They found that they were received more warmly and were able to get through many more presentations with fewer objections.

So a credibility statement works like the proverbial "stitch in time that saves nine." In fact, a number of the tips in this chapter will function the same way: to prevent hassles and customer resistance.

INSTRUCTION 4:
REMEMBER, THE BEGINNING *IS* THE "MEAT" OF THE CALL

One of the reasons telemarketers pay so little attention to how they start a call is that they think it is relatively insignificant when compared to the actual offer they're going to make, which usually comes later.

How foolish! Unless callers can get to the offer, they haven't accomplished anything. The beginning of the call *is* the meat of it, to the customer. It is during this time of making a first impression that you are selling yourself.

Prospects are asking themselves, with each passing split second:

- Do I like this person?
- Can I trust her?
- Is she going to waste my time?
- Will I miss something important if I end the call now?

In other words, a lot rides on how well callers do in the first several seconds of the contact. If telemarketers fail at this stage, they can forget about wowing listeners later, because there won't *be* a later!

CONQUERING SECRETARIAL SCREENING AND VOICE MAIL

When you're doing business-to-business calling, and even some consumer calls to residences, you need to be proficient at getting through a gatekeeper in order to earn the right to communicate with the decision maker. If there is any single hurdle most telemarketers fail to clear, it is getting through secretaries and other lions-at-the-gate.

I have good news for you. You can double your effectiveness by making a few changes in your approach. I'm happy to tell you that these alterations will be polite and professional.

You won't have to lie to anyone, and you can feel completely good about the process. Before I get into the new techniques, you need to see the problem telemarketers currently have with the process.

Right now, phone salespeople are innocent lambs who march off to slaughter. No kidding! The reason is simple: We use traditional, hand-me-down methods of starting calls.

Here's a typical exchange between a screener and a caller:

Hello, Acme Baskets, how may I help you?

May I speak to Bill Smith, please?

Who is calling?

Bob Jones.

And your company, Mr. Jones?

Jones Construction.

Does Mr. Smith know you?

Uh, no, not really.

Perhaps, I can help you?

Uh, no, I'd rather speak to him, if you don't mind.

I'm sorry, that won't be possible. He's not available at the moment. May I take a message?

This has all been very conventional stuff, am I right? This is an ancient script for failure, which 99 percent of salespeople use!

Why? I apologize if this sounds self-serving; but until I came along, no one had devised a better one. But before we explore it, I need to point out *why* the traditional one is such a perennial loser.

- **Screeners use a great script.** Think about it: All the cards are neatly sorted and then stacked just right, so screeners will win, call after call. By setting the call up as an interrogation, where they play the role of Questioners and sellers are Answerers, they have an immediate advantage. They make callers passive, while they remain active.

- **Sellers have conferred great power and status on screeners.** Sellers *expect* to be pummeled, shaken up, and generally trashed. So they actually sound timid when they call.

Have you ever seen a lost dog scurrying through a strange neighborhood? Head and eyes dart all over the place, and he seems to want to be anywhere else. That's what most callers sound like when they encounter screening. No wonder they lose!

- **Screeners are used to winning, to beating back callers, until they submit with a whimper.** Screeners are on a roll, so to speak, and when you have the momentum in your favor, you transmit a power signal that intimidates your adversaries — the callers.

- **Salespeople have become a "conquered people."** They start believing the negative stereotypes that their captors propagate. They start believing that their products aren't so good, after all. And what right do the callers have to disturb busy executives with calls that they aren't expecting? (The answer is they have every right to call because their products are going to HELP the business people they are contacting!)

- **Sellers have never been let in on the big secret.** Screeners are bullies, so when you stand up to them — politely, professionally, and firmly — they back down.

As with every tip I give you in this book, I expect you to put what I'm saying to the test. I assure you the techniques I'm about to give you *will* work. They're simply awesome.

So, here's how we rewrite the screening script to make it a winner for you rather than for the screeners. Please note that I called it a script because it is, and I urge you to use it word-for-word. (Some other parts of the call can be improvised, but not here!)

The first thing to do is change how callers introduce themselves in the call. They don't ask, "May I speak to Bill Smith, please?" In fact, it is a major mistake to ask at all.

One of the great, and generally unwritten, rules of communication is this: If you wish to get information, *give* information first.

This especially applies to phone calls. After all, why should listeners tell callers the whereabouts of a colleague if they don't know you? Indeed, to ask them to do so, which is exactly how traditional telemarketing operates, is impolite.

Callers shouldn't put people in the position of forcing them to disclose what could be sensitive information to outsiders. So, callers are polite by telling listeners who the callers are right away. The opener is:

> Hello, Gary Goodman, Goodman Communications, for Bill Smith please, thank you.

This is an extremely important and effective opening if it's delivered properly. For proper delivery, callers need to orchestrate what I call the Three T's: text, tone, and timing. First, let's examine the text, and I'll explain why it's so powerful.

By telling the screener who callers are, and the name of their company, telemarketers have eliminated the need for the person to ask. So they've done the listener a favor, which saves time. By disclosing, first, without interrogation, callers made his or her job easier and less stressful.

After all, who likes phone squabbles? Psychology also says that when people self-disclose, they create trust. (The converse applies, as well. When people *conceal* information, they arouse distrust and suspicions, which result in rejections.)

But there is an even more significant impact that this Opener has — it throws the screener off of his or her conventional script! This "deskills" the person, but in a friendly, likable way, so it is hard for the person to come back at callers as an Interrogator. (Some will try, but you'll see how to handle it, believe me!)

Look at the text closely to see whether it passes the test for a suitable opener: Is it polite, professional, and firm? I think you'll agree that it is.

What's polite about it? Several things. It starts with a friendly *hello*, then a *please*, and concludes with *thank you*. Selling doesn't get more polite than that!

The style is professional because the callers have disclosed their name, the name of their firm, and the name of the person with whom they wish to speak, all in a time-managed way.

But it's also *firm*. What do I mean by this? To appreciate this dimension, you need a tip for handling your tone.

Here's the instruction: Start with a high tone, and then stair-step downward until you reach a low tone at the end of the phrase. So *hello* is high on the tone chart, whereas *thank-you* is very low.

It's as if you are stating a fact — not asking a question.

If you "ask" this phrase, instead of stating it, you'll make the screener smell blood in the water, and there will be some ugly thrashing, believe me.

If I were to give you an "attitude" with which to convey the line, it would really entail three shifts. First, you're friendly, with *hello*. Then, you're businesslike with your name and your company name. By the time you say *thank you*, you should sound almost bored, and not overly eager.

Because screeners aren't prepared for the feast of information you're providing them at the beginning, they may ask you to repeat yourself. This is great! They'll often say, "I'm sorry — would you repeat that, please?"

It's great, because the screeners are apologizing to *you*! This represents a major change in how they're accustomed to dealing with callers, I can tell you! All you need to do to keep the good feelings going is to respond with, "Sure."

Then, slowly restate exactly the same opener that you used before, but this time, end it with, "Thank you *again*."

By this time, if you've had to repeat yourself, the screener may feel an obligation not to hassle you, and your call may be put through. But a number of screeners will bounce back and will try to pick up the tatters of their script with this fragment: "May I tell him what this is about?"

At this point, many salespeople become defensive. They grit their teeth and improvise an unsatisfactory answer. Usually, it fails.

Please prepare this line as carefully as you would your opener. This secondary screening line is just as important. Here are three possible responses:

- "Certainly; it's about our recent correspondence, thank you."

- "Sure; I've been asked to extend a personal invitation to her, and I'll be happy to hold, thanks."

- "Of course; it's about our recent corporate communications, thank you."

Again, let's put these options through our polite, professional, and firm test. Is each phrase polite? No question about it. In each line, we endorse the right of the screener to play his or her role by asking for that bit of information. We say, "Certainly," or "Sure," or "Of course." Believe me, screeners really appreciate this treatment!

And these exchanges end each line with words of appreciation, with thanks. How could callers be more polite?

Are these professional? Sure they are. Callers succinctly deliver the requested reason for the call.

And are these firm? Yes they are, because they punctuate the conclusion with "thanks" or "thank you." They're firm, because they send a metacommunication, an "above-message" that implies, "Now please go get her and don't give me any back talk!"

But they do it ever so nicely, right? That, my friend, is a part of its great power.

What if the screener still feels feisty and says: "Perhaps I can help you?"

This is when salespeople are tempted to lose their patience, but as you can appreciate, they can have infinite patience because they're going to win. So callers respond this way: "I wish you could, but I've been asked to speak to her directly, and I'll be happy to hold, thanks!"

Isn't that lovely? "I wish you could …" This says the caller likes the screener and is sending a very nice, affirming, relationship message to the person.

By this time, believe me, the caller will be put through. Even if the caller were rebuffed or the person were unavailable, the caller as well as the screener will both feel much, much better about the exchange. And the caller will be much more likely to be put through the next time.

Before you think this screening management method applies exclusively to business-to-business calls, I should point out that the same method works beautifully in calling households.

Let's say you call Judy Smith's residence, and a man answers the phone, and to make things interesting, let's say, you're a male, as well. If you ask, "Is Judy there?" you may arouse some defensiveness if you're speaking to a jealous friend, significant other, or spouse.

But if you begin with, "Hello, Gary Goodman, Goodman Communications, for Ms. Smith please. Thank you," you'll get a much better reception. It will sound like the business call that it really is, not a personal contact. (The same principle applies if a woman caller reaches a woman but is asking for a man; as well as in same-sex scenarios.)

CONQUERING VOICE MAIL AND ANSWERING MACHINES

Screening isn't the only challenge telemarketers face when they begin telemarketing calls. Voice mail and answering machines have become nearly universal, so let's explore how to deal effectively with them.

How do people use voice mail and answering systems? They're a big help to people who are busy or who are out of the office, right? They permit folks to get their messages and to return calls when it is convenient. In fact, the odds are good that you use some sort of message-taking device, as I do.

But when we're selling, they can be very frustrating. A machine can't say "Yes" or award us a sale, then and there, as a person can. But just as I gave you methods for getting through screening, there are several ways to deal with voice mail and answering machines.

YOU CAN LEAVE A MESSAGE!

This is terribly obvious, right? But messages will vary in quality and in impact. If you're cold-calling, how likely is it that a prospect will call you back if you say you're *selling* something or if you give that impression? Not likely at all.

I received one of these messages at my office the other day:

> Hello, I'm with Acme Printing Industries and I've been receiving your brochures for some time, and I would like to speak to you about your printing business. My name is Bill Smith, and my number is 555-5222.

Did I call him back? I have to admit I didn't, because I don't have time. Moreover — and this is ironic — I had already been doing business with this fellow's company, which filled my last order for 70,000 brochures!

Most folks, unless they're on the verge of getting printing bids, won't call this guy back, because they don't have the time, either. So, leaving the kind of message he left for me, what I call the Gee, I'm Just a Salesman Doing My Job! message, generally isn't worth his breath.

There are circumstances, however, when leaving short voice mails can pay off. First, the messages need to be short — 30 seconds or less. Second, you need to script them (here I go again, with that S word!). And they have to have a few additional elements.

One element is urgency. The fellow from Acme Printing injected no urgency into his message, right? If he said the printers were having a special sale for a limited time, and he asked for a return call the same day, well, he'd be in much better shape.

That kind of statement would get someone like me to focus on his offer. I'd take it seriously, and I'd ask myself, "Do I have any printing I could do right now?" I *do* have some letterhead and envelopes that I could reorder and stockpile. But his actual message left me cold and unmotivated.

WHAT IF YOU LEAVE A MESSAGE THAT'S "TOO GOOD"?

I'm often asked to write a voice-mail script that'll enable salespeople to leave such a brilliant message that most prospects will immediately call them back.

Without a wonder script, most salespeople are lucky to hear from 10 percent to 20 percent of those with whom they leave a recorded message. That's a pretty dismal result, which makes sellers wonder whether they're wasting their effort.

After all, it takes time and energy to stop one's work flow to leave these pleas. The question arises, would telemarketers be better advised to skip the messages, keep dialing and smiling, and then to pitch the prospects who are at their desks, ready to chat?

That is my main instruction: If you're cold-calling, *don't bother leaving messages* because:

- If you just leave your name and number, people will suspect it's a sales call, and they'll resent calling you back.

- Your message will probably induce the prospect to say No based on insufficient information.

But there's an even more potent reason for not leaving messages. What will happen to your work process if a lot more prospects suddenly started returning your calls? Would you be ready to handle them?

This challenge was faced by a recent client of mine, for whom I had written a dynamite voice-mail script. Returned calls surged from about 10 percent to 50 percent, overnight.

This is just what the client had dreamed about, but it turned into a nightmare. How come?

- Reps weren't able to accept the return calls because they too were busy making outbound calls.

- The return calls went into voice mail, so the prospects who had called back were needlessly frustrated.

- Even if reps were able to handle some of the calls, switching from a proactive, outbound frame of mind to an inbound, more passive frame of mind was jarring and ineffective.

There was a silver lining that the client and I discovered in the form of an insight. We had learned to work more *efficiently*, but we weren't more *effective*. We needed to overhaul our assumptions and processes about the role voice mail messages played in the sales cycle.

After interpreting our new results, we decided to stop leaving voice mails for all cold prospects. This came as a welcomed relief to salespeople, who could now concentrate on reaching only those people who were accessible.

The moral: Watch out what you ask for — you may get it. But even if you do, you may gain an even better perspective into the role of that outcome in producing or in frustrating sales.

YOU CAN BREAK THROUGH
VOICE-MAIL SYSTEMS RIGHT NOW,
IF YOU'RE CLEVER

I'd like to offer a more fruitful approach that can help you to avoid leaving messages altogether. You see, I use the phones to sell my products and services, so I hit the same potholes any business-to-business salesperson encounters.

Let's take a deeper look into how our prospects use their voice-mail systems. Of course, they block out unwanted calls, but they can also prevent desirable calls from getting through.

To avoid that, users tell their friends and family how to defeat their electronic sentries. If someone really wants you to reach her, she'll probably give you an instruction like this:

"Call me, and if you get my voice mail, hit the Operator key and have me paged."

Guess what she has probably told the operator:

"If someone asks to page me, it's okay; I'll pick it up."

So, the operator presumes that it's safe to page people without being criticized.

That's great news for salespeople and for folks who don't want to be rebuffed by voice mail. When you get someone's messaging system, do exactly what a friend or family member would do.

Push *O* and say, "Would you please page Bill Smith? Thank you!"

Notice that your request begins as a polite question, but it ends as a statement that sounds "final." By inserting "Thank you!" you'll metacommunicate to operators that they needn't ask you who you are.

Even if they do, it's easy to mention your name in a similar way: "It's Gary Goodman, thank you."

Using this technique, I've been successfully bringing people to the phone at double my previous rate. These are folks with whom I've had no prior contact, and my sales are surging as a result.

Are there any downside risks in using this new gambit? I haven't encountered any. I'm always ready for someone to say, "You paged me for *this?*"

Then again, I do contact a number of sales and marketing executives, so they may actually admire my ability to get their attention.

I attribute my success to the fact that even if my prospects don't know who I am, they've still committed to the operator and to friends and family that they will answer their pages. So, I'm simply circumventing the voice-mail system that they have already voluntarily disabled.

Try it for yourself, and let me know what you think!

Now that you know how to conquer secretarial screening and voice mail, you're on your way to making the perfect telemarketing call. You've begun well, and now your objective should be to keep your forward momentum going.

I'll show you exactly how to do this in the next chapter, as we explore the exciting psychology of successful telemarketing.

CHAPTER THREE

THE PSYCHOLOGY OF SUCCESSFUL TELEMARKETING

I may be the only person on planet Earth who ever *wanted* to be a telemarketer. This isn't a normal wish for most kids, many of whom long to be firefighters, writers, sports stars, or computer experts. But I saw, or should I say I heard, my calling early on, right in my own home.

In a sense, telemarketing was the family business. My dad was a great salesperson. He set sales records wherever he worked, and a large measure of his success was attributable to his phone skills.

He liked to make calls from home, in the morning, and then visit his prospects in the afternoon. And was this guy smooth! He had a pleasant speaking voice, and his words seemed to come together effortlessly.

He seemed capable of relating to all kinds of people. Sometimes, he'd adopt a slight inflection in his voice if he was speaking to someone who sounded that way. At other times, his voice would become almost a whisper, to match a prospect's low-key delivery.

Because his sales were so high and he never seemed to come into the office, the source of his selling power was invisible to his rivals and even to his managers. Dad liked it that way. He reveled in pulling rabbits out of hats, so to speak, and he confided to me that the real source of his power came from the phone that he cradled in his hand.

Compare this exposure that I had to telemarketing, which was obviously positive and encouraging, with the way most folks are introduced to this business. Their initial impression is often quite negative. As I mentioned in the first chapter, most of us identify telemarketing as an inferior way to communicate with prospects because many of our experiences as customers are poor ones, from a qualitative point of view.

Because we have come to feel telemarketing is flawed, we think it must *continue* to be that way, even if we become the telemarketers. And of course, that's simply not true. Telemarketers have a great opportunity to improve the standards of this medium, as well as the results it yields. But the first job is to delve into the psychology of telemarketing, so we'll look forward to our phone work, instead of shunning it.

Let me share a story with you that exemplifies how people *can* feel about telemarketing. The other day I was phoned by a reader of one of my other books. He had retired from U.S. government service, and he was looking for a part-time supplement to his pension. I sensed he was still relatively young.

As it happened, he lucked into doing telemarketing for a consultant who wanted appointments with CEOs so he could sell his services to their firms. My reader was paid $100 for each appointment, and he averaged setting about five of them per week. It took him only about 20 hours to do, so his pay worked out to about $25 per hour.

Naturally, he was happy about this, and after the consultant's "dance card" was filled, the retiree went on to offer his services to other companies on a contract basis. He purchased some of my advanced training tapes, but before he did, he asked me: "Do the tapes talk about how much *fun* telemarketing is?"

Well, I was taken aback, I have to admit. I suppose I had come to expect that people would be at least a little sour about using the phone, but this fellow was quite the opposite.

He was having a great time — a peak experience, if you will. His enthusiasm made me remember my first phone jobs and the thrills I got from making successful calls.

After high school, my first office job was as a telephone debt collector. I was one of about six people who reminded customers of a finance company to pay their bills. I succeeded almost right away.

What amazed me was the fact that the people I phoned took me seriously. They actually sent their payments in! You see, I wasn't used to grown-ups taking directions from me. In fact, I had a baby face at the time, so I would have been much less persuasive if I had asked them to do anything face-to-face.

The phone was like a magic carpet or a genie in a bottle. It transported me from being just a teenager into being an effective member of the business world. I can't tell you how heady an experience that was.

It was one thing to have watched my dad perform over the phone, but when I had done it, I truly came to *own* this medium. What a great tool!

The next year, I "graduated" to doing telemarketing work for Time/Life Books. The thrills were amplified for me because I started making good money, when sales commissions were factored in. I got so good that I was promoted to sales management, and my telemarketing career was officially launched.

So, it can be great fun transforming yourself into a telemarketer. I found the fact that I was "only a voice" to customers to be a big plus. By being audible but also invisible, I could sound any way I pleased and be judged based on what customers heard but didn't see.

IDENTIFYING PHONE FEAR

Some people have the opposite feeling. They're held back by what I call "phone fear."

When I was doing a seminar in Indiana, a big, burly, and outgoing salesman shook my hand and told me how he suffered from tremendous call reluctance whenever he had to make appointments for himself by phone. Of course, who would have expected that such a commanding figure of a man would be afraid of a little phone?

But I had seen phone fear before as a sales manager and as a consultant. And this fellow reported experiencing all of its symptoms: sweaty palms, shortness of breath, and an urgent desire to do anything else but make calls.

We spoke for about 45 minutes because I wanted to help him and to explore this psychological handicap. At one point, he revealed something very important.

He said: "I feel that I know how I'm doing when I'm selling someone, face to face, but over the phone I have no idea about how they're reacting to me."

In other words, the absence of visual feedback from the client made the salesperson feel threatened and insecure when he communicated by phone. This concern has now been echoed to me by many salespeople, so I know it's valid.

Contrast this experience with another one that I've observed. You remember the finance company I told you about, right? Well, there was the sweetest, elderly lady who worked there who actually wore her *bedroom slippers* when she was in the office, and she was quite a sight as she'd shuffle back and forth to the copy machine.

This lady was timid when her office mates would speak to her, but when she got on the phone, she transformed herself into a dynamo. She was a "skip-tracer," which is a telephonic bounty hunter. She had the task of tracking down "deadbeat debtors" who had disappeared, usually across state lines.

Over the phone, she was bold and relentless. Like the Canadian Mounties, she normally found her quarry. But to speak to her face to face, you'd never suspect she was such a powerhouse. She had two completely different personalities.

So what can we conclude? Big, outgoing guys can shrivel up on the phone, while diminutive, fragile seniors can thrive? Yes, that's part of the message. So please don't prejudge your telephone talent or that of other people. You could find the phone to be your "best" communications and selling medium.

But If You Do Suffer from Phone Fear, There Are Remedies

But at the same time, there are a few "fixes" for phone fear that are guaranteed to work: (1) Using positive imagery, and (2) using systematic desensitization.

Remember what our big salesperson reported? He was afraid because he couldn't *see* a person's feedback over the phone. This led him to fear that he was dealing with sourpusses, so he would start sounding weak and downcast, which would result in the very rejection that he feared.

I urged him to substitute an image of a happy, supportive, head-nodding prospect for the dour, negative, and head-shaking portrait that he normally maintained when he telecommunicated. That would lead him to expect success from his calls, and in doing so, he'd be likely to sound like a winner while promoting victories instead of failures.

The second way to tame phone fear is to use systematic desensitization. This means you should do as much of what you fear as is possible.

The person who fears heights should ride elevators all day long in the tallest skyscrapers. The new driver who fears freeways should spend as much time on them as possible while mastering entrances and exits.

And the phonophobic should make as many calls as possible. In each case, scared individuals will see that they survive the experience and their worst fears never materialize. Which leads me to the next magical, comforting question.

WHAT'S THE WORST THING THAT CAN HAPPEN TO YOU?

You may recall that President George Bush was visiting Japan and having a formal dinner with that country's prime minister when he suddenly was overcome with stomach flu and ejected his meal onto the lap of his host.

Yes, that made the evening news, and it seemed to be one of the most humiliating moments in the history of state dinners. But did Bush survive the embarrassment? Of course. (I'm not so sure about his victim!)

I was a college professor for five and a half years, and one subject I taught was public speaking. You may have heard that people's fear of giving a speech outranks their fear of dying.

Having evaluated hundreds of student speeches, I never had one presenter faint at the podium or require the services of a paramedic. Were they scared? Sure. A certain amount of stage fright is normal and to be expected. But it can be managed.

SMART PEOPLE LEARN TO CHANNEL THEIR FEARS

Successful speakers tame fear by transforming it into helpful emotions, such as exhilaration and enthusiasm. Instead of allowing their imaginations to offer up images of defeat and humiliation, they conjure up images of victory and wild acceptance of their ideas.

It isn't that winners never experience fear — to say that would be an utter lie. Many of the best performers and the most successful telemarketers get the butterflies. But they don't dwell on the chances for failing. Instead, they concentrate on executing the mechanics of succeeding.

For instance, the public speaker rehearses her outline so she feels increasingly comfortable with the flow of ideas contained in the speech. The salesperson or telemarketer does the same thing, anticipating how to handle questions and interruptions when they arise.

I used to instruct my students to prepare their introductions carefully and to invest more time with these first ideas than with any other part of the presentation. My theory is that when speakers feel 100 percent confident in their initial subject matter, they'll do well with it. And this early smooth entry into the topic will enable speakers to relax through much of the remainder.

PHONE FEAR, LIKE STAGE FRIGHT, IS MANAGED — NOT CONQUERED

No matter how experienced you become as a telemarketer, don't expect to ever banish the butterflies entirely. It hasn't happened in my lifetime, and I can assure you, I've made lots and lots of calls.

There have been long periods of time during which I've been off the phones. I have had extensive consulting contracts or I was teaching instead of doing. Or I've been writing articles or books, so making calls has been only an intermittent activity for me.

During these "dialing doldrums," I've experienced a resurgence of phone fear. It has taken the form of self-doubts about my ability to come across in top form. When I allow myself to maintain these concerns, they grow and fester, and before long I can find myself procrastinating.

So I postpone calling, which only makes we wonder more whether I still "have what it takes." There is only one cure for this problem, and that is forcing myself to climb back into the saddle and ride.

YOU CAN'T BE PERFECTIONISTIC AND
SUCCEED IN TELEMARKETING

Of course, before I get back on the horse, I have to accept that there will be some bumps on the trail. I may even get thrown and land, unceremoniously, on my butt!

That's life, and I have to remind myself that perfectionism only leads to more procrastination and to self-contempt. You see, I have to battle perfectionism because I am a well-known telemarketing "expert." Gee, it's easy to think, I should be perfect and earn every sale, right?

Wrong. No one is perfect, and I have to keep reminding myself of this fact. Even a pro can't win 'em all, and no one can earn each and every sale. In fact, continuing in the face of setbacks is one of the things that every professional does every day!

If you have never tried to telemarket, you're probably going to be concerned about failing and about embarrassing yourself. You'll do a little of both. So what? The worst thing that can happen is people can reject your message.

Big deal. Believe me, it has happened before and it will happen *again*. I suppose it is one of the glorious aspects of being in business that telemarketers don't have to be perfect and have a flawless, 1.000 batting average to succeed.

If they win only a small percentage of the time, they'll be fine. In telemarketing, most programs that I've been a part of have worked on an 80/20 principle: callers get about four "no's" for every "yes." This, in baseball terms, means you can bat only .200 and win!

This is approximately the law of averages when it comes to appointment setting, as it is for a number of other telemarketing-related activities. So if one in five, or better yet, one in four prospects say yes or perform as you would hope, you'll be in pretty good shape.

SET YOUR EXPECTATIONS AT THE PROPER LEVELS

When we're kids, we constantly try new things because everything is new to us. It's a pleasure to discover novel things to do, different foods to taste, and new places to visit.

But as adults, we turn into reactionaries. We'll often insist on being guaranteed that we'll be satisfied before we'll try anything that's out of the ordinary. I encounter this risk-averse attitude among people I interview for telemarketing positions.

They immediately want to know who is the top salesperson, how much she's earning, and any other details I can convey. Their interest is in determining, "Is the game worth the effort?" In other words, are the rewards here?

But their real questions are these: Will I succeed here? Can I make it? Do I have what it takes? Referring to the experience of another person who is already aboard will never give them the assurance of success that they crave. Because there is only one surefire way to tell if someone is going to make it as a telemarketer, and that is by having the person get on the phone and try.

It's interesting, isn't it? I can get rusty through inactivity and revive my own phone fear, and what's the remedy? That's right, getting on the phone and calling my way out of it.

What's the best way to tell whether you're going to succeed in telemarketing? The same way: by getting on the phone, taking your chances, and seeing how you do.

So how should you set your expectations? The best tip I can give you is to expect to learn, period. You'll probably fail in the beginning. Even if you're following a script, you'll lose your place and have to improvise until you can return to where you left off.

You'll mispronounce people's names, and they'll correct you. Some prospects will sound like speech coaches as they admonish you to "Slow down, darling. Now, that's better."

All of which is the stuff of learning, if you choose to perceive your experiences that way. If you expect to have your ego satisfied immediately based on achieving stellar results, you'll probably be disappointed.

In a sense, you would be better off expecting *not* to get sales right away. That way, you'll stay humble, accept in stride the inevitable rejections that come, and carry on until you succeed.

WHAT WAS THAT I SAID ABOUT "REJECTION"?

Rejection comes with the territory. Expect it. You wouldn't anticipate playing tackle football without smudging your uniform, would you? It goes with the game. Sometimes you'll have absolutely no impact on the results you get with given prospects.

For instance, the other day I answered my business line and a telemarketer introduced himself. He went on to say he was with an accounting firm that specializes in working for consultants. Instantly, like a reflex, I said, "Well, we have an accounting firm, thanks. Bye!"

Within 10 minutes, I regretted having dispatched the caller so quickly. It occurred to me that it would have been wise to check the company's billing rates and references in case I wanted to change firms. But I had barked out my rejection of his message so swiftly that I didn't even hear the firm's name!

So, instead of being upset that I was called, I was disappointed in myself that I didn't see the call as an opportunity. I certainly wasn't rejecting the caller, as a human being or as a business person.

My response had nothing to do with *him*. It had to do with *me*, and with the abrupt mood I was in at the time he called. It's important to remember that as you make your calls.

Rarely will people be rejecting *you*, personally. In fact, that's a strength of the phone, if it's an audio-connection and not a video-connection. We appreciate its impersonality.

If someone saw your image on a video screen, he or she might be inclined to put on a happy face and lead you to believe there was true interest when there was no interest at all.

In that sense, a quick rejection is a plus because you won't waste your time following up with a prospect who only told you he had interest in order to get off the phone gracefully. By swiftly eliciting a "no," you're statistically closer to reaching someone who will say "yes."

Now, I would be less than accurate if I told you that no one will be rejecting you, personally. There are too many incidents of personality clashes that have occurred in the annals of telemarketing for me to make that claim. You just won't meld with certain people, or they with you.

But you will find most people are reasonably polite, and some will be encouraging and enthusiastic. I heard a salesperson say that her task was "finding buyers" more than "persuading people to become buyers."

What did she mean? There are many positively predisposed prospects out there, who are virtually *waiting* for your call. They *want* to buy what you're selling.

If you allow yourself to become discouraged by the nonbuyers, you'll probably never reach enough of the enthusiastic people to sustain you in your career. Let me make an analogy to direct mail marketing that should bring this idea into greater focus.

There are two kinds of copywriters in direct marketing: (1) Those who write their copy for buyers, and (2) those who write it for nonbuyers.

The ones who aim at buyers usually write lengthy sales letters that go into great detail about the products or services being offered. The other kind of writer practices her craft defensively. Her goal is to try to get fewer recipients to toss her writing into the trash when they discover that they're holding solicitations.

She'll focus on using jazzy headlines and clever teasers to induce people to read further, and she won't "bore readers" with details.

Who is more successful? In my experience, it is the writer who aims at buyers. Buyers crave details. They're encouraged by long descriptions because they need a good justification to do what they're already positively predisposed toward doing — buying.

Readers who don't want to buy, especially by mail, won't be converted by flashy headlines and teasers. They may be amused temporarily, but the mailing piece will still go into the trash.

Because you're about to telemarket, I suggest you concentrate your mental and emotional efforts on buyers and not on nonbuyers. Just as you have to peel a shrimp to eat it, you need to go through an outer layer of nonbuyers to reach the nourishing buyers inside.

MAKE A GAME OUT OF BEING REJECTED

I know a bond salesman who went for nearly 11 months without making a sale. Then, in November 1993, he made a memorable conquest: He sold a $100 million investment to a bank. His commission exceeded a *million dollars.*

Was it worth being rejected for nearly an entire year to be rewarded later on by a huge commission? What do you think?

Would you put up with "a whole lot of nothing," as he did, if you felt that you could get a big commission later for your efforts? Most people, surprisingly, wouldn't. They would opt for a "guaranteed" return on their investment of time. How come?

It seems less risky. Who knows? They could go for 111 months without earning a single sale, right? So they don't want to starve in the meantime.

But there is a more profound reason people would be threatened by an all-or-nothing, straight-commission pay plan, such as the one that made a millionaire out of the bond salesman. Most folks are ill-equipped to handle the reinforcement schedule that a straight-commission pay plan ushers in.

The salespeople just can't stand the idea of working hard for a long, long time without seeing results. I suppose they wouldn't make very good farmers, either. They'd plant their seeds in the fall, worry all winter, and absolutely disbelieve that they'd see sprouts in the spring.

The bond salesman felt secure in the belief that his exertions would pay off, and they did. On a smaller scale, if you wish to succeed in telemarketing, as he did, you should to learn to postpone gratification.

Appreciate from the get-go that it may take you a while to earn your spurs in phone work. Although I believe the Almighty is generally kind to novice telemarketers, while seeing to it that they get some positive feedback early in their careers, there is nothing to ensure that this will happen to you. (I'm being a big comfort here, aren't I?)

One way to ease your anxieties about dealing with an infrequent reinforcement schedule is to create a reward schedule of your own. Let me give you an example.

I'm writing this book, obviously, a word at a time. But if I thought about the duty of writing a 58,000-word manuscript one word at a shot, it would seem like a daunting task. Instead I break it down into different reward-units, as many writers do. John Grisham writes one page per day, so a novel takes him about two years to complete. All he concerns himself with each day is that one page.

If he grows concerned about what the characters will do a hundred pages from where he is, he'll simply waste his time and become deskilled.

By creating one page at a time, I have found that the book will finish itself, just as a farmer's seeds will sprout and the bond salesman's calls will become transformed into sales.

After a day's work, the bond person shouldn't look at himself in the mirror and say, "Gee, another day without a sale." He has to tell himself, "What a great day of building a base from which future sales will come!"

I suppose it boils down to a matter of having faith and of keeping your hand to the plow. Faith is defined as fostering "belief without proof." We believe that our ministrations will culminate in sales and in a successful career. But we don't have any guarantees.

The farmer's seeds could lie frozen in the ground and never sprout, but that's unlikely. If you work hard at telemarketing and commit yourself to being diligent and to continuously improving your craft, you will succeed. I have faith in that.

One game you can play with yourself is called "Counting Rejections." Bizarre as it may sound, you can set aside a pen and paper and make hash marks on the page each time someone rejects your message. Then, when you get a sale, pause for a moment and do a little math.

Did it take 10 rejections before you earned a sale? Good. Now you have an idea of how many times you may have to hear a "No" before you'll hear a "Yes." When you get back on the phone, you can cheerfully "thank" people for their rejections because you'll know, from a statistical standpoint, they've just helped you to make 10 percent of the progress it takes to earn a sale.

TELEMARKETING OFFERS HIGH "PSYCHIC INCOME" AND GOOD "PERKS"

There's a lot of psychic income to be earned in telemarketing. I'll explain.

One of my primary values is independence. It runs in my family. We really like to feel we're in charge of our own destinies.

Telemarketing has always made me feel that way. I can sell anything by "smiling and dialing." I can also do it from anywhere in the world, as long as I can get a dial tone.

To me, that independence of career equates with freedom and the ability to call my own shots. If you examine the classified section of any city newspaper, you're bound to find positions available for telemarketers. I'll grant that some aren't the best positions, but nestled in the newsprint you'll be delighted to discover that others are decent.

Looking at the same paper, you may not find any positions for lawyers or professors, which are occupational titles that I have also earned. The sales profession is unique inasmuch as it has few educational entry barriers or other requirements for breaking into the field. You can enter it or leave it at will.

As long as there is a market economy, there will be jobs available for salespeople and, I might add, for telemarketers. This means that you can have mobility and not have to worry about being unemployed — at least for long.

When I was teaching college, part-time, and working on my Ph.D., I found that I wasn't earning anywhere near the money I had earned as a telemarketing manager a few years before. So I went to the college career center and saw an ad to sell office products by phone.

I got the job by picking up the phone, in front of everyone, and by making a strong sale with my first call. What gave me the self-confidence to try that straight-commission job?

I knew I had good phone skills from my prior work in telemarketing, so I simply transferred my book-selling methods to selling ballpoint pens. By having an income supplement to go along with my teaching salary, I was able to buy a new car and maintain a comfortable lifestyle while my fellow graduate students merely subsisted and complained about their lot.

TELEMARKETING CAN OPEN A LOT OF DOORS

David Geffen is the billionaire who founded Geffen Records and is a principal in the film company Dreamworks. His career began in the mailroom of the William Morris talent agency.

As he would shuffle along with his mail cart from one agent's office to the next, he'd try to listen to how agents plied their trade. He observed one crucial thing: The successful ones were *always on the phone!*

When he was promoted to agent status, he set a goal for himself to make 200 phone calls a day. Certainly, some were brief, but his key to success was staying in touch through this medium.

Geffen used telemarketing to become a billionaire.

There are numerous professions in which the phone plays a prominent role, though practitioners aren't called "telemarketers." Stockbrokers and investment advisors perform most of their client communication work by phone. So do lawyers, when they aren't researching or making court appearances.

When I've recruited literary agents to represent my book projects, I've violated the accustomed practice of writing them notes regarding their representation. I've thought through a brief summary of who I am and where I'm headed, and I've picked up the phone and called them.

I can't tell you how powerful phone skills are in everyday life, whether you're trying to get vital information from government offices or simply trying to make reservations for New Year's Eve at a solidly booked restaurant.

When you know how to telemarket, you'll be providing yourself with an advantage that will pay off for a lifetime. Knowing this is very rewarding psychologically.

TELEMARKETING INCLUDES COLD CALLS AND A LOT MORE

When you think of telemarketing, what comes to mind? Do you see a frazzled person calling utter strangers, one after another?

This is certainly an accurate portrait of cold-calling. Cold calls are really aimed at making "new" contacts. Some people feel that this is the hardest type of telemarketing one can do, and, in the main, I agree.

For example, today I made some cold calls into the office machine industry. Frankly, I encountered a lot of suspicious people on the other end of the line. These were mom-and-pop outfits, which apparently don't receive many out-of-the-blue solicitations.

If your first task in this field is to make cold contacts, you're going to need to brace yourself for some abrupt conversations. Some prospects feel they owe cold canvassers no duty of politeness or civility, so they don't mind being rude.

At the same time — and this is the wonderful aspect to cold calling — you might just stumble into people who were thinking at that very moment of buying exactly what you're offering. When I was in the car-leasing business, which I entered after the book business, I chose to make cold calls to build a client base.

My manager thought I was nuts. "I really don't think you can lease cars by phone, Gary," is what he told me. But that's the method I used, and sure enough, within a few weeks I found a fellow with a small business who needed not one, but two new cars!

I was thrilled, and my accomplishment became an instant legend. Before long, all new account executives were expected to cut their teeth in the business by making cold contacts.

I've actually found five benefits to making cold calls, even if you're established in the telemarketing field, as I am.

- **The hardest thing about making cold calls is deciding to sit in a chair and simply do it.** It's easy to procrastinate. But you'll feel proud of yourself for making the calls after you've gotten underway, and this enthusiasm will spill over into your personal life. When you can make cold calls, you'll feel you can accomplish anything!

- **Cold-calling is a fast and cheap way to determine whether you've chosen the right target for your marketing efforts.** For instance, I set forth to call a number of financial services executives who I thought would be receptive to buying my audio seminars. They were, but as it turns out, approximately 25 percent of their phones are disconnected. Apparently, there is so much turnover in their ranks that getting a current and cost-effective list is nearly impossible.

  I'm grateful that I made some cold calls before investing in an expensive mailing!

- **If you get an extremely poor reception to your efforts, you've probably made a marketing error.** You could be speaking to the wrong people in organizations or be going after the wrong types of organizations. Cold calls enable you to make this judgment fast, then correct for it.

- **After you do cold-calling, you'll be a complete tiger when you are dealing with warmer leads.** Cold calls sharpen me so much that I can really appreciate the leads that I've obtained from other sources, such as inbound inquiries. I've relearned the value of jumping on warm leads instantaneously. My deal-making percentages soar with warm leads after I've been dealing with the frostier variety.

- **You'll appreciate the value of your existing clients when you have to do "ice-fishing" for new ones.** Moreover, you'll be more inclined to ask your current customers for referrals because you'll recognize that an introduction of this type almost always ensures a polite, if not enthusiastic, reception.

Most telemarketers avoid cold-calling whenever they can. But by doing so, they cheat themselves out of an experience that makes callers sharper and more appreciative salespeople.

OTHER FACETS OF TELEPHONE SALES

But as I mentioned, cold calls are just one component of telemarketing. This field also includes simple data gathering and list building.

Let's say I need to contact senior executives in companies, and I can't obtain their names from conventional list brokers. I could be forced to compile my own list, and the telephone is a great way to build this resource.

One of your first tasks in telemarketing might be doing just this, or you might be asked to *clean a mailing list* by confirming names and titles through phone calls. From a psychological standpoint, this is a nonthreatening task, and your greatest mental obstacle in performing it might be having to fend off boredom.

But there is an advantage to starting out in the field in this manner. You'll speak to a lot of people, and you'll learn how to be succinct and persuasive with those who may not want to reveal information. You'll be assimilating core telemarketing skills that will grow so that you'll be able to take on greater challenges.

Telemarketing also includes making *appointment calls* on your own behalf or for sales executives. I'll provide you with some powerful language for setting appointments in the next chapter. For now, take my word that this is a fairly easy task, as well. In appointment setting, you're not really asking for the final buying decision. You could be setting the stage for that, but you'll find that there really isn't that much stress involved.

Account qualification is another task that is very low-key. You may find that you're asked to *qualify leads* that have come back to a company from an ad it ran or from a trade show its representatives attended.

Before sending out an expensive mailer, your firm may want to separate the wheat from the chaff to see who has real interest and who is not a good candidate for further sales activity. So your job could be to call all the leads, ask them key questions about their interests and buying capabilities, and then pass this intelligence along to management.

I know several professional telemarketing service agencies that do no "selling" at all. In fact, they avoid it if they can, because they know it is difficult and they can use the phone to make money by taking on less ambitious tasks.

You can always manage your psychological comfort level in telemarketing by doing exactly the same thing. If you like, go to work for firms that use the phone in a way that makes you comfortable.

For example, some companies do business-to-consumer phoning. You may like this, or you could prefer business-to-business calling. Or, you may want to receive calls in an inside sales or an order department, and not make any outbound contacts.

It's really up to you.

You Can Impact How You're Rewarded

I mentioned that many folks have a tough time dealing with the reinforcement schedule that can apply in commission-based sales. When you live from sale-to-sale like this, your income can certainly feel less than secure.

But you don't have to work in a straight-commission environment. Although some of the jobs you'll see advertised in the newspaper pay representatives based on performance alone, most do not.

Steady Wage Plans

You'll find that telemarketing pay plans differ dramatically, and there is probably one form of pay that will mesh nicely with your personality. For instance, some telemarketing jobs pay a steady hourly or weekly wage.

This makes a telemarketing job feel much like any other form of office work. Now if you're a real spitfire and you achieve at high levels relative to your peer group, a flat salary may leaving you feeling, well, flat.

You'll find that your pay raises normally lag far behind your increasing levels of achievement. This can breed frustration and resentment, when you see that you're the best salesperson but your pay is equal to that of the lower producers.

But if you want a reasonably low-stress telemarketing job, look for one that pays a guaranteed wage of some kind. By receiving a salary, you'll see that much of the emotional risk in doing telemarketing work is being diminished, and that's great for many people.

Salary Plus Commission

A variation on this pay scheme is a guaranteed salary plus a commission based on achievement. I think this is the best of both worlds. You have security, so there is a financial safety net that will protect you if your sales are in a free-fall.

But if you do produce, you'll not only get your guarantee, but you'll also get a nice "spiff" on top of that, in the form of commission. This plan is great for people who need a basic feeling of assurance as they undertake a new form of work but who catch on fairly fast and are looking to do very well after that.

In some sense, the pay plan that you negotiate will really be similar to the risk-vs.-reward model to be found in financial investments. If you put your money into a government-guaranteed savings account, then your rate of return on that investment will be low.

If you invest in a jazzy new company that has an innovative product or service, you may get a spectacular return on your bet, but you could also go bust if the industry doesn't live up to its promise. In telemarketing work you'll probably find that the preset wages are modest, but commission percentages can be very high.

For example, I'll pay my sales reps anywhere from 20 percent to 40 percent of the gross dollars we generate from product sales. This can mean exceptional earnings for reps who are hard working, sharp, and lucky enough to hit paydirt early in their tenure with me, so they stay motivated.

But I also remember a fellow who worked hard for about three weeks and made only one solid sale, for a commission of $100. That worked out to about $1 per hour for his efforts. Before you think that I benefited from this outcome as his employer, let me set you straight on that.

Yes, I would have been out of pocket even more money if I had been paying him even the minimum wage. But I was out of pocket for phone costs, office overhead, training, and supervision time. I lost a lot more money than he did.

I say this to point out that telemarketers should seek a pay structure that balances the risks and rewards for all parties. And as the Oracle of Delphi once said, it pays to "Know Thyself." Give thought to which type of pay structure is the most rewarding to you, financially and psychologically, as you shop for positions in telemarketing.

Should Telemarketing's Image Problems Concern You?

Telemarketing is a global business, and every indication I get is that it is just going to keep on growing. So from the standpoint of "being in the right place at the right time," I think you are there, right now, if you're entering this field.

One of my colleagues opened an executive-recruiting firm in telemarketing a few years ago, and his business is going great guns. He tells me that pay packages are soaring for telemarketing executives, and that many salespeople who set up large calling campaigns for telephone service agencies earn annual incomes in the six figures.

Our society celebrates people who earn the big bucks, and it is just a matter of time before the status of people who excel in telemarketing increases. Status tends to follow power and money.

Moreover, telemarketing is becoming a high-technology business. If you enter a large telecenter, you'll be amazed by the equipment automation that is constantly being upgraded. State-of-the-art centers will be multimedia Meccas, linking callers and prospects by the Internet and using real-time, two-way, multiparty video conference capabilities.

Frankly, such centers of technology are becoming high-status, glamorous places in which to work. I'd hate to be the sales executive of tomorrow who wants to justify catching a flight to visit prospects across the nation or the world.

Her manager is bound to ask, "Why not dial them up and have an instantaneous and meaningful video call here and now?" (Earlier this year, I sold the last share of airline stock I had in my portfolio!)

TELEMARKETING OFFERS ALL THE
PSYCHOLOGICAL REWARDS YOU MIGHT NEED

The "meaning" we derive from our work is really a function of our attitudes. If we expect to be disappointed by our career or by an occupation, we will be. And we'll also be rewarded if we expect to be.

Martin Luther King put it well when he said:

> If a man is called to be a street sweeper, he should sweep streets even as Michelangelo painted, or Beethoven composed music, or Shakespeare wrote poetry. He should sweep streets so well that all the ghosts of heaven will pause to say, "Here lived a great street sweeper who did his job well."

If you substitute the word *telemarketer* for street sweeper, you'll appreciate how I feel about telemarketing.

I've actually tried to leave this field. I've been a college professor and I am an attorney. But I keep coming back to telemarketing because I've found it has everything I need — spills, chills, money, fun, variety, and a lot of mobility.

And I can't tell you how much joy I get from creating something out of nothing. That's just what happens when we *Reach Out and Sell Someone!*

I hope you come to feel the same way about it.

In the next chapter, I'll show you how to structure your outbound conversations so they're productive and enjoyable.

CHAPTER FOUR

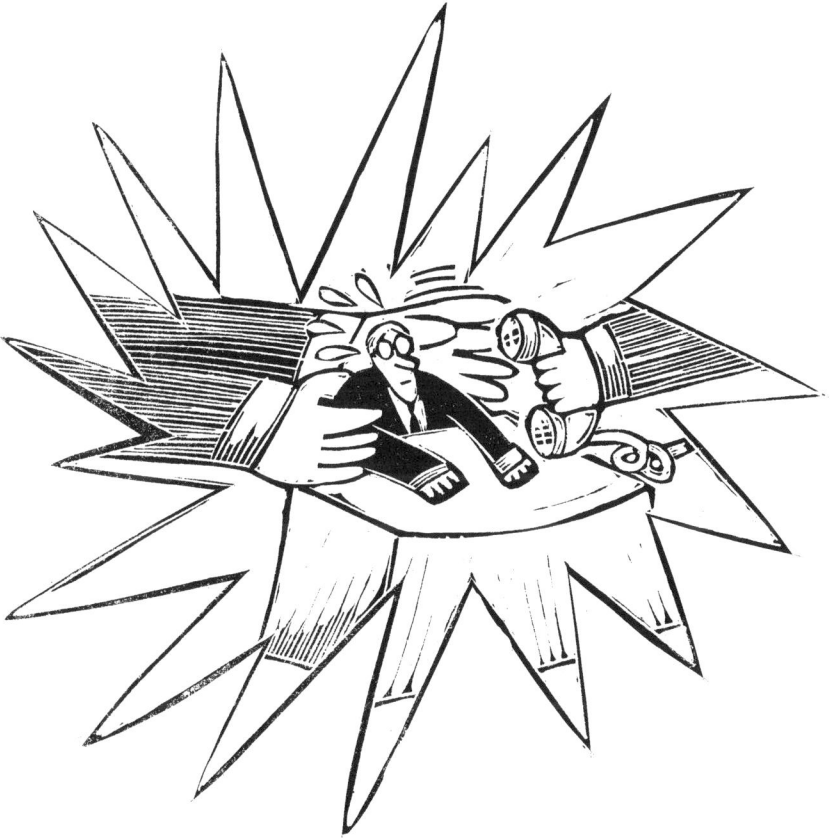

ANATOMY OF AN OUTBOUND TELEMARKETING CALL

There are many ways to put together an outbound telephone sales call. I'm going to share two approaches that I've found to be successful. The first is the traditional method, and second is the New Telemarketing method.

Throughout this book, I've made a point of saying that the new way is superior, in my estimation. It is built on two-way conversational principles, which are generally more agreeable to both buyers and sellers — but not always.

There are circumstances when you'll choose to — or even be compelled to — use the older ways, so I'd like you to learn them. The traditional way also has strengths, and if callers are smart, they'll try to adopt its pluses while leaving its drawbacks behind.

So, my purpose in this chapter is to give you multiple tools and to show you when it is appropriate to use them.

SALES "PRESENTATIONS" VS. "CONVERSATIONS"

It might be helpful to distinguish the two respective approaches to telemarketing this way: You can think of them as either presentations or as conversations.

Traditional telemarketing adopts the presentational mode, whereas the new school uses a two-way, conversational mode. Frankly, you may be more comfortable doing most of the talking, or presenting, as you begin your telemarketing activities. If so, you can always evolve into using the more conversational way after you've chalked up some experience.

STRUCTURING THE PRESENTATION

No matter which method you start with, your sales talk will need to be structured so you can manage your time as well as make sure that you're using a consistently productive and persuasive message. A traditional sales presentation has all the components of a traditional a story or a speech: a beginning, a middle, and an end. Over the phone, these elements have traditionally translated into a four-part sequence, consisting of an opener, description, close, and confirmation.

This four-part structure is valuable because (1) It still works in producing certain types of sales, (2) some prospects even "request" it, and (3) you can "cannibalize it for its parts" when you do conversational selling.

What do I mean? First, let's say you're trying to sell a commodity, such as plastic kitchen trash bags. These are items that nearly everyone is familiar with. People know how they're used, their features, and their benefits.

A one-way pitch that says, "We have what you need, and here's the price," may be all you need to engineer agreement. If you've ever hung out with salespeople or their managers, you've undoubtedly heard this expression: Keep It Simple, Salesperson. (There is a more insulting version of this KISS acronym, as well: Keep it Simple, Stupid.)

The KISS method aims at teaching sellers the lesson of simplicity. It is a valuable one to learn. KISS is at the heart of the one-way method of selling, especially when you're promoting well-known products or commodities.

Some prospects who you call will want you to cut to the chase when you tell your sales story. Imagine phoning a buyer who interrupts you in the middle of your credibility statement and who gruffly demands, "Okay, what do you want?"

I wouldn't advise using anything other than KISS when you hear this type of person. Similarly, if a prospect challenges you with: "Why should I buy this widget?" be prepared to react with a direct answer, where *you* do the talking.

Finally, you'll find the traditional format is useful because it can be cannibalized for parts, just as a junked automobile can be stripped of its remaining assets.

Here's what I mean. The traditional sales pitch has some valuable components. For example, it gives you a number of ways to open your talk so you don't have to fumble for words. It also forces you to select certain features and benefits of the product to explain. Typically, you'll preselect the features and benefits that you believe are appropriate for the majority of prospects.

It will also compel you to learn certain formulas for eliciting agreement from customers. These are known as *closes*. And traditional selling will often require you to use confirmations to ensure that your customers realize what they are buying.

All of these are valuable functions that traditional selling serves. However, you don't have to use it in its entirety. Feel free to take from it what you believe will be valuable and keep in mind that it pays to be flexible in adopting a selling style.

But enough preliminaries. Let's get into the mechanics of this four-part method for structuring your outbound telemarketing calls.

PART I: THE OPENER

An opener is your reason for contacting the customer, today. There are several that come to mind:

The Thank-You Opener

The thank-you opener is used when someone has done something for you or your firm. She could be a customer who bought something recently, or even long ago. This ice-breaker warms people up by showing appreciation for their patronage.

A thank-you can also be given to someone who sent in a business reply postcard to learn more about your services. Of all the openers, I think I like the thank-you opener the most because it creates a positive atmosphere and promotes the relationship between the buyer and seller.

The New Product/Service Opener

This opener is known to all of us. Someone calls us or walks into our place of business to tell us about an innovation that's going to change life on planet Earth as we know it. The word *new* is almost always a great attention-getter. If this word didn't work, it wouldn't appear on so many products in the supermarket.

The Demonstration Opener

This is the give-away method of selling. It's also known as "Try it, you'll like it," selling; it relies on giving someone a free taste of or sample of a product. If you're selling carpet-cleaning, you might call prospects and offer to clean one room of their house for free to show how effective you can be.

The Inactive Account Opener

When companies haven't communicated with a customer in a long time, this opener can be especially effective. They've stopped buying, and we've stopped selling. It is a good way to remind someone that the company exists, while discovering why he may not feel he needs the product or service any more.

The Special Sale Opener

Almost everyone appreciates hearing about special sales on items that they customarily buy. But some of these calls come as surprises, though pleasant ones.

For example, I nearly fell out of my chair when my jeweler used the special sale approach over the phone to sell me a unique bracelet for my wife. Naturally, he mentioned how he was discounting it!

Special Occasion Opener

The jeweler not only called to tell me about the discount, but he knew it was our anniversary. (Talk about pressure!) Thus, he had combined two openers, the special sale and the special occasion, and that's perfectly smart to do. His particular approach also showed superior marketing savvy — he knew my needs and really was performing a service.

The Urgency Opener

"We lost our lease!" is a classic example of the urgency opener. I'll say this: It gets people's attention, and it almost has a built-in incentive to get them to buy, *now!* Think about it for a second. If a retailer phones to say she lost her lease, she's not going to be around very long, is she? So the customer thinks, "I'd better get over there and pick something while the picking's good!"

Retailers realize how powerful urgency is, and for this reason, many of them will place deadlines on buying. For example, they'll announce "eight-hour" sales that get people's attention and bring them in, pronto.

The Referral Opener

After announcing your name and that of your company, you might say: "Our mutual friend, Bill Smith, asked me to call you." If you did this, you'd be using the referral approach. If your prospect has high regard for old Bill, he'll probably transfer Bill's halo to you, and he'll welcome the opportunity of speaking to you.

But watch out if he doesn't feel that good about his old buddy, Bill Smith. I was given two referrals a while ago to people who seemed to completely disrespect the referral source! Needless to say, I stopped using her referrals.

The New or Sudden Idea Opener

Sometimes, telemarketers get a sudden inspiration. For example, I had been courting a prospect for two years when it hit me that I had just signed up another client in her region. I phoned and mentioned the coincidence, and that led to adding my long-sought-after prospect to my collection of clients.

Occasionally, you'll simply get an inspiration where there's less of an obvious reason to call. You might contact a prospect and remark: "I was reading the newspaper and suddenly, I got an new idea that I thought you'd be interested in." I sense that people are grateful to hear that salespeople are thinking about them, so the new or sudden idea approach works. Plus, it's actually refreshing because it sounds so spontaneous.

The Affinity Opener

This opener announces your shared affiliation right away, as the ice breaker. "Bob," you might say, "I'm calling you as a fellow USC graduate … ." This works in much the same way as the referral approach. If the person you call thinks highly of USC or the affinity group you mention, you could be in good shape. If he's a UCLA fan, you could be in big, big trouble!

The Description: The Second Part of Your Call

Once you have opened the call, the next step is to get into the meat of the presentation. This is when you mention your product or service while sharing some pertinent details about it.

Let's say you're selling a membership to the local art museum. What will you want to say about it? You should mention certain crucial details about the term of membership and the benefits that come along with it. Before people can agree to buy, they need to know what they're getting, right?

Be very selective in what you say. After all, you might be capable of discussing hundreds of beautiful art objects a patron could enjoy, but then the talk would last forever.

You should choose only a few *especially attractive* items, and mention them concisely. You should try to boil your description down so that you cover only two to four benefits.

This would be a good time to review the difference between features and benefits. A *feature* is usually some objective characteristic of a product or service. "We have 100 Impressionist paintings in our collection" is really mentioning only a feature of your product.

But by saying, "You'll have a chance to appreciate all the subtle aspects of Impressionism through our ample, 100-piece collection," you have stated a *benefit*. You have told the buyer what the 100 Impressionist pieces mean in terms of the value he or she will derive from seeing them. Try to remember the following saying when you write the descriptive part of your presentation: *People buy benefits, not features.*

So, always try to translate a feature into a benefit and you'll be more persuasive.

THE THIRD PART OF YOUR CALL: THE CLOSE

Closing a sale means getting the person to say "Yes" to your offer. It is an important moment in the selling process, and for this reason some salespeople place great emphasis on learning as many closes as they can.

To some extent, this part of the presentation is overrated. If you have done a wonderful job with the first two parts of your talk, the opener and the description, people will be leaning toward buying anyway.

So you shouldn't have a great need to use a powerful gust of persuasion to close sales when a mild breeze will do it, or when customers simply choose to close themselves.

Nonetheless, it is useful to learn how to close because many of the people you call will not close sales themselves without at least a little nudging from you.

There are three kinds of closes that work for me: (1) the choice close; (2) the assumptive close; and (3) assumptive-checkback close.

The Choice Close

The choice close has been around forever. It was the first one many of us learned as kids. In fact, our parents used it on us when they asked: "Would you like to clean your room or give up your allowance?"

That's not much of a choice, is it? This homey example is intended to point out that the "choice" in the close is often illusory. We're not giving people time to reflect on the alternatives we're presenting them. We're allowing them only a moderate feeling of control over what or when they buy.

The classic illustration of the choice close is when it comes from a car salesperson's lips: "That convertible sure is good looking in the blue — or would you prefer the red?"

The customer's impulse is to jump in and to state a preference: "I'll take the blue!"

That's what sales lore predicts the customer will do, all the while feeling that he or she made a forceful decision.

The power in the choice close is created by giving customers a choice between something and something, not something and nothing.

If you wanted to persuade someone to spend time with you, it might not be wise to ask, "Would you like to go out on Saturday night?"

This innocent-sounding question almost asks for rejection. Never, ever, do you want to put a prospect into the position of being able to utter a flat, nearly impossible to recover from, "No."

So, you'll probably fare better by asking your closing question this way: "Would you like to get together on Friday night, or would Saturday be better?"

By offering a choice, you lessen the chance that the answer will be a complete rejection of your idea. Again, you're not asking, "*Do* you want to go out?" Instead, you're asking, "*When* would you like to do it?"

The choice close may seem a little hokey, but it has actually proven itself to work for decades. But I should warn you: Avoid overusing the choice close — or any type of close, for that matter.

Some foolish salespeople reach for the same type of close again and again, with the same prospect, during the same conversation.

Let's say our "date" target, in the example just described, replied to the initial choice close with, "I'm busy on Friday and on Saturday."

We wouldn't want to offer a string of additional choices: "How about next Friday or Saturday? Or the following Tuesday or Thursday?"

After a while, the choice close can sound gimmicky, and it will fail on that ground, irrespective of the buyer's wishes to do what you're asking.

To help you to avoid overusing any one close, I'll supply you with two more closes, which I've found to work very well.

The Assumptive Close

When using the assumptive close, you are making the decision for the prospect. This works especially well when you're trying to get fence-sitters, or indecisive types of people, to buy. Often, they're risk-averse, and no decision is too small for them to sweat bullets over.

Sometimes, I need to use the assumptive close with my daughter when we go to McDonald's, as in "Honey, would you like the chicken nuggets or a burger?"

Occasionally, she freezes up; her eyes are fixed on the toys being offered in the Happy Meal display case. I repeat the choice. I get a dazed gaze in return. Finally, I take the lead and declare: "You're getting the chicken!"

I know this seems a bit brusque. Let's polish it a little and apply it to a sales situation. You're on the phone with a prospect with whom you'd like to set a meeting. You try the choice close: "The calendar indicates a good time to stop by will be Tuesday at 10, or will Wednesday be better for you?"

The prospect replies that neither will work out. You say, without missing a beat: "Okay; let's just make it Thursday at 10. I see you folks are located at … ."

By following the declined choice close with an assumptive one, you'll sound decisive, and you'll have a good chance of being granted the appointment.

The Assumptive-Checkback Close

There is a third type of close that works very well, and I use it often. It's called the assumptive-checkback close. This close combines the assertiveness of the assumptive close with a sense of choice. So it is like a hybrid close.

Let's say you want to get a person to order a product by phone. You might close the customer this way: "So, let's get this widget out to you, and I know you'll be pleased, okay?"

If you delivered the entire phrase, while leaving off the last word, okay, it would be a strictly assumptive close. By checking back with the person for an endorsement, you're softening an assumptive close without sacrificing its effectiveness.

It's easy to remember how to fashion an assumptive-checkback close: Simply make a declarative statement, and stick an "Okay?" at the end.

So, give this close a try, and I know it'll work out for you. Okay?

If you would like an alternative for "Okay?" you can try "Fair enough?"

I suggest you memorize a few assumptive-checkback closes. This way, you can use them as the right opportunities develop. Here are several versions of it:

- Sounds good, doesn't it?

- And that's nice, isn't it?

- That's great, don't you think?

You're getting the hang of it, aren't you? I told you that you could do it, didn't I? You get the idea, don't you?

Other Closes That Deserve Honorary Mention

I believe that you can get considerable mileage out of the three main closes that I've provided, but there are a few others that I should acquaint you with.

One of them is the *"Where Did We Go Wrong?"* close. Here's the situation. You've tried every means known to the sales world to get someone's business. You flopped, blew it, struck out.

I suggest you try giving these prospects a little breathing time. Let them think you are gone, forever. Then, call or write. Here is the text of a letter I've used, which can be easily adapted to the phone:

> Dear Prospect,
>
> I would like to thank you for having given me the opportunity to be of service.
>
> Unfortunately, it seems that I may have let you down in some way, because I didn't earn your business.
>
> As a marketing professional, I would benefit from hearing how I went wrong or may have missed the mark. Any feedback you could offer will be most appreciated. I have provided some space below for your comments, along with a stamped, return envelope.
>
> Thank you for your assistance.
>
> Sincerely,
>
> Gary S. Goodman

Approximately one in three deader-than-dead prospects will respond to an approach such as this. When they do, they'll usually revive the buying process.

This happened to me a few years ago. I reached a dead end with a prospect and sent the note. Within three weeks, someone else wrote me back, indicating that she was the true buyer.

Within a short time, I was awarded a national training contract!

I would also like to recommend the *"Ben Franklin" close.* You may recall from grade school how old Ben would make a list of the pluses and minuses of a proposition before taking action.

He'd simply choose the side that had more entries. You can help a prospect to make a logical choice by having him or her write down the pros and cons of your offer. Then, ask the prospect to count the respective entries. By the time the customer sees that the "aye's" beat the "nay's," you have earned a sale without seeming to pressure the person at all.

So far, this chapter has covered the first three components of an impersonal sale: the opener, description, and close. Now, we'll explore the final component, the confirmation.

THE FOURTH PART OF YOUR CALL: THE CONFIRMATION

After you have opened, described, and closed, it is advisable to walk the prospect through a confirmation. This brief segment of the conversation recaps the agreement that has been created.

Specifically, you want to go over fulfillment details. How will the prospect receive her product or service, and when? Will it be shipped via UPS or sent by mail, and how many days will it take to arrive?

Once again, how many products did the person agree to buy? Five gross? And what is the unit price, and the total price, including shipping and handling?

One of the main reasons you need a confirmation is to create mutual clarity. No one needs to have a misunderstanding about a material part of the agreement.

After the buyer says, "Okay," I like to start confirmations with these words: "Fine. Just so I'm clear, we'll be shipping your order to … ."

I put the emphasis on my clarity, not the buyer's. This is a nondefensive way of saying that everyone needs to be clear before the sale can move forward.

It is also important to provide for unanswered questions. Before disconnecting, I make a point to ask: "And is there anything else I can help you with?"

This way, if there are misunderstandings, you nip problems in the bud and you're able to emerge from the selling transaction with the firm belief that the sale will "stick."

Some sellers from the old school are afraid of using confirmations. They believe that you should "close and run." Once the prospect has okayed the deal, get the heck outta there!

I don't buy this idea. If you're so afraid that your sale is shaky, you shouldn't bother writing it up. Cancel it yourself. Don't delude yourself into thinking that it is anything other than weak.

Here's why. It is always more costly, emotionally and financially, to cancel a sale later rather than earlier. After time elapses, you and your company have gone out of pocket. Commissions may have been paid. Products may have been scheduled for manufacturing or purchase.

You and the people who believe in you, such as your family and your sales manager, have been led into thinking that you've scored when you haven't. Undoing deals later is a bad thing for your ego.

Either firm up a sale with a confirmation moments after it has been made or cast it aside. You could say a confirmation is an important reality check of your sale's strength.

Moreover, the confirmation gives the prospect an "out" if you applied too much pressure, or if he or she said yes just to get off the phone. It's a safety valve that I believe is necessary when you elect to use the traditional style of telemarketing.

EXAMPLE: A TRADITIONAL TELEMARKETING PRESENTATION

It's important to see how the four parts of the traditional call come together, so this scenario shows you how simple this format can be. Here's an example of a presentation that aims at selling kitchen trash bags.

> Hello, Mr.Ms. ———— . I'm Gary Goodman and I'm with Clean & Neat Industries. You've probably heard of us — we're the largest producer of kitchen trash bags, like the kind that you probably have under your sink. How are you this afternoon?

> * * *

> Good. The reason I'm calling is to tell you that we're having a special sale on our yellow plastic kitchen bags that come with the convenient twist-tie attached to the side of each bag. You're probably paying as much as 18 cents per bag in the supermarket. We're offering them in a convenient box of 250 at only 5 cents apiece, which is an unbeatable price.

What we're doing, to help folks to get acquainted with us, is sending out our orders on a completely guaranteed basis. If you aren't completely impressed with the strength and value of our bags, you can return the unused portion, at any time, for a refund. That's how confident we are that you'll really like them.

So, let's get a box out to you, and I know you'll be pleased Okay?

*   *   *

Fine. Just so I'm clear, we'll be sending you a box of 250 yellow kitchen bags at a price of only 5 cents apiece. That comes to a total of $12.50, and we'll be paying for delivery, okay? Would you like to put this on a charge card, or would you prefer to pay by check? ... Okay, great, you'll receive your bags in about five days, and are there any questions I can help you with?

*   *   *

Well, fine, and I'll include a catalog of our other discounted home and kitchen supplies, okay? Well, thank you, and have a good day! Bye.

Let's do a quick checkup on the four parts of the call. Did you hear them? I hope so! What was my opener? That's right, it was the special sales approach.

What were the two benefits that I mentioned in the description? If you said the "convenient" twist-ties and the low price, you're right.

Which close did I use? That's it — the assumptive-checkback close. And did I repeat the essential terms of the offer and delivery details in the confirmation? What about asking the customer if there were any questions — did I do that?

You may have noticed a few other touches. I used a credibility statement at the beginning of the call that positioned my company as the largest producer of bags. And at the end of my confirmation, I set the stage for follow-up sales by mentioning the catalog that I was sending out that contains additional values on other items.

So, this is the essence of a traditional telemarketing call.

Now that you have seen this method in action, let's move into learning more about the new and more conversational school of telemarketing.

THE NEW TELEMARKETING

It's one thing to *claim* that the New Telemarketing is different. I want to *demonstrate* it to you, and you'll have options in the selling style that you adopt. So indulge me a little as I list the ways that this new, conversational method differs from the traditional way of telemarketing.

CONVERSATIONAL SELLING ENCOURAGES EFFECTIVE COMMUNICATION, NOT JUST EFFECTIVE PERSUASION

We're really trying to see the world as prospects see it: Where are their opportunities? What competitive threats do they face? What are their problems today, and how can we prepare them to meet tomorrow's needs?

When I was speaking to some executives at the auto club, I tried New Telemarketing. Although I was primarily concerned with one aspect of the club's member communications, I asked this question to get a more global perspective on their marketing situation: "To what extent is the club concerned about other organizations that are starting to provide emergency roadside service?"

This single question unlocked some important information that helped me to see how the organization viewed its current and future mission. By asking this question, I was able to anchor our discussions to the priorities of the organization. I can't overestimate the importance of communicating effectively with the "whole" prospect or firm in this kind of way.

CONVERSATIONAL TELEMARKETING RELIES ON THE USE OF QUESTIONS MORE THAN STATEMENTS

Instead of telling your way to a sale, the New Telemarketing emphasizes the process of *asking* one's way to a sale. This doesn't mean that the only thing you do is ask questions — far from it. But you almost always try to *ask* before you *tell*. This reverses the customary sequence.

Traditional telemarketers don't bother asking questions until their presentation starts hitting reefs. If it's smooth sailing without probing for information, why bother?

Or so they think. Questions are mighty powerful tools in helping you to customize a presentation.

It's equally important to ask questions because they get the prospect involved in a conversation. When a prospect becomes involved, he or she takes responsibility for the success of the encounter.

The customer then helps you to succeed. Instead of watching while you perform, as if you're a fish in an aquarium, the customer is swimming in the conversation with you.

You've heard the Biblical suggestion to "Ask and you shall receive," haven't you? It really works in building relationships and sales.

There are four types of questions you should use in telemarketing: (1) open, (2) narrow, (3) closed, and (4) leading. By forming your questions in careful ways, you'll elicit valuable information in return.

I'll describe these questions in detail a little later on. Suffice it to say at this point that these questions distinguish traditional telemarketing from conversational by giving you techniques for getting prospects to talk and to gladly reveal their needs to you, so you can satisfy them.

NEW TELEMARKETING STRESSES A "WE" ORIENTATION

Instead of a seller-centered, "Me, Me, Me" approach, the New Telemarketing tries to create a win/win solution with the client. Translate this ideal into economic terms. Win/win selling promotes the idea that the buyer should receive top value just as the seller should receive a healthy profit.

Let me give you an example of a win/win business relationship that I have with one of my vendors. I do a considerable amount of direct-mail marketing. The firm I use to design the "look" of my brochures isn't cheap. And yet, its overall contribution to my success is substantial enough to justify continuing our relationship. In other words, taken as a proportion of my overall mailing expenses, the design firm's cost is minor.

Surely, I'm paying the firm top value for its work, but I'm getting value in return. I suppose it's just one more example of getting what you pay for.

THE NEW TELEMARKETING APPROACH SEEKS CUSTOMER COMMITMENT, NOT JUST A FINAL "YES"

Commitment implies several incremental levels of persuasion, and I believe this term captures more closely what callers are trying to achieve in an interpersonal selling scenario.

Commitment, in New Telemarketing, substitutes for the "close" in a traditional call. Sometimes it is inappropriate to ask customers to buy if they don't know enough about you or your product. But you still want them to commit to building a buying relationship with you.

For a number of months my wife and I were actively searching for a larger house in a town with a well-regarded school district. The days were counting down until my daughter needed to begin kindergarten, so you could say we were really motivated to buy.

We specified to the Realtor exactly what we wanted: a house with character, a large yard, and a certain amount of interior space. Realtor after Realtor showed us homes that didn't even come close to this description.

I'll never forget one of the places we were shown. It was on a steep hillside instead of having a level yard! After we looked at it, the Realtor abruptly tried to close us by asking, "What would you like to offer on it?"

My wife and I were exasperated. We had zero commitment to the place, and the Realtor didn't have a clue because she was busy closing when she should have crafted a mutual commitment with us to pursue our specific buying objectives.

NEW TELEMARKETING INVOLVES TRUE "MARKETING" AS WELL AS SALESMANSHIP

Marketing is defined as all the activities necessary to "create a customer." An example may help to illustrate the distinction between marketing and salesmanship.

Right now, I am writing these words while sitting at my favorite restaurant. I just watched a customer wait near the front door for 15 minutes to speak to a manager to find out whether the establishment could sell her an extra portion of its unique salad dressings.

After the manager came out, he flatly told her, "Sorry, we don't sell them that way." Predictably, she walked away, feeling very disappointed.

I happen to know for a fact that this restaurant hears the same request dozens of times every week. What should that be telling the management? Bottle the dressing and sell it separately, because there is a big profit to be made by giving customers what they want!

The manager here acted in a traditional way. A traditional salesperson sees the task as selling only what he has on hand, the traditional way, and not necessarily what will truly satisfy the customer. Marketing is always hunting for, or at least receptive to hearing about, the unsatisfied needs that can be served.

INTERPERSONAL TELEMARKETING IS USUALLY LOW-KEY AND LOW-PRESSURE

The distinction between telemarketing styles almost speaks for itself. If you're trying to push someone into buying, you're not operating in a New Telemarketing mode. Using too much pressure breeds resentment, very little repeat business, and even fewer referrals. So, it is usually self-defeating.

TRADITIONAL TELEMARKETING IS DEFENSIVE;
NEW TELEMARKETING IS SUPPORTIVE

Defensive messages include evaluation, control, strategy, neutrality, superiority, and certainty.

Supportive messages, by comparison, involve description, a problem-and-solution orientation, empathy, spontaneity, equality, and flexibility.

Once I bought a European sports car from a snobby dealership. When I returned with a repair question, the salesman defended the manufacturer of the car while using defensive communication. He said: "Why, these cars are smarter than most people!"

He was obviously calling me a dummy, which is the essence of evaluation, a defense-producing message. By doing this, he took our focus away from problem solving, and our conversation could have deteriorated into a name-calling contest.

Conversational telemarketers focus on creating supportive interactions while reducing or avoiding defensiveness in any way they can. They try to catch themselves before they make huge interpersonal blunders.

IN NEW TELEMARKETING, THE CUSTOMER BECOMES ACTIVE INSTEAD OF REMAINING PASSIVE

The customer usually feels that she is a vital partner in the conversation every step of the way. Most importantly, customers feel that they're buying instead of being sold.

WE BECOME INTERDEPENDENT WITH CUSTOMERS WHEN WE ADOPT A NEW TELEMARKETING STYLE

We need customers to inform us about their needs, and they need us to help them to fulfill them. Instead of playing a game of hiding needs, customers tend to open up to us so we can help them to buy.

WE SUBORDINATE OUR SHORT-TERM SALES GOALS FOR LONG-TERM RELATIONSHIPS AND ENDURING PROFITS

It has been said that when customers feel goodwill toward a supplier or seller they represent "annuities." In other words, it's like money in the bank for you when buyers look forward to buying from you again and again.

The traditional seller only sees this moment's dollar value of the customer. He or she ignores the person's long-term potential, which can be substantial.

For example, I have used the same accounting firm for more than 20 years, through good times and bad. When times turned tough, as they have more than once during those years, if the firm didn't moderate its fees and services, I wouldn't have been able to afford to retain it. If we had parted company, the firm wouldn't have benefited from the upswings in business that followed the slumps.

Now that I've outlined some of the critical differences in traditional vs. New Telemarketing, let's look at how the new process works on a step-by-step basis.

ANATOMY OF A NEW TELEMARKETING CALL

The conversational sale usually follows these five steps:

1. Opener.

2. Probing.

3. Discussion.

4. Focusing.

5. Commitment.

Right away, you may have noticed that this format differs from the traditional approach in some important ways. It adds two crucial steps: probing and focusing. It also ends with a commitment step.

But it also has some similarities to traditional telemarketing.

Your openers will be exactly alike in both forms of telemarketing. The discussion section, as you'll see, also has some similarity to the description in the impersonal sales structure.

So, you'll see that we're recycling some of what you've just learned about traditional selling while augmenting it in some important ways.

PROBING

What, exactly, are telemarketers probing for? They're looking to uncover unsatisfied needs that their companies' products and services can meet.

Specifically, sellers want a prospect to say the equivalent of these three things as they move through the probing section:

- I have a need.

- It's important.

- And I want your help in satisfying it.

When a telemarketer can get a prospect to say these three things, the caller will have accomplished 80 percent of the sales mission.

How do salespeople get customers to say these things? Sellers have to ask their way to that result.

I have found that the following sequence of probes gets people to tell sellers what their needs are:

1. Callers should ask about customers' current circumstances. What product are they using now? How is it working out for them?

2. Callers want to find out how customers' current methods aren't satisfying them. What is the gap between what they want and what they currently have? This is the unmet needs step.

3. Callers want to ask customers about the importance of this unsatisfied need to them.

4. Callers want to ask prospects if they would like telemarketers' help in satisfying it.

So, callers probe for circumstances, unmet needs, importance of the needs, and customers' desire for telemarketers' help. In doing so, telemarketers are using a motivated sequence for persuasion that is comfortable.

Sellers are following a problem-to-solution pattern.

You might be wondering, why bother with all this probing if my company already has a good idea about what customers' needs are?

Sellers probe because people like to express their needs and prefer not to have a stranger tell them what they are. Through self-disclosure, customers not only buy a company's products but also buy into the experience of working with the brand.

People become truly committed. And this makes them loyal customers because they identify with the telemarketer, the company's items, and the firm's sales methods.

EXAMPLES OF NEW TELEMARKETING

EXAMPLE 1: PROBING

A number of my consulting clients sell financial services and investments. One firm has identified affluent, older investors as its market. These individuals are drawn to investments that have low risk but an above average financial return. Typically, these investors put their money into interest-paying accounts and Treasury bills.

Because there is no urgency that drives these investors into the arms of brokers, telemarketers need to probe to develop a current motivation to change customers' investment allocations.

Conversational telemarketing would have a broker introduce herself and her company, and then the conversation might go this way:

Broker: What kinds of investments are you attracted to now?

Investor: I have my money in CDs, and municipal bonds, mostly.

Broker: Savings accounts, too?

Investor: Yes.

Broker: How are today's lower interest rates affecting the performance of those investments?

Investor: Well, I'm not getting what I used to get, I can tell you that!

Broker: How much less of a return are you seeing than, say, six or seven years ago?

Investor: I used to see about 8 percent, and now I'm lucky to get 6 percent.

Broker: So, your return has dropped by 25 percent or more?

Investor: I guess so.

Broker:	Is that meaningful to you?
Investor:	Sure.
Broker:	How has it affected your lifestyle?
Investor:	I can't afford to visit my grandchildren as often as I'd like.
Broker:	If I could show you some ways to get a higher return on your investments without sacrificing safety, would you like to explore them further?
Investor:	Definitely. What do you have?

I'm sure you can see how comfortably this conversation develops. It sounds like there's some good give-and-take to it, right? It's designed to sound that way. Let's review what we did in this example:

1. The broker got some vital information about the investor's current practices with a circumstances question.

2. The broker elicited an unmet need by asking how today's lower interest rates have affected the prospect.

3. Next, the broker performed an important clarity check to determine whether the prospect felt the need was important.

4. Finally, the broker asked whether the prospect wanted to pursue the satisfaction of the need with the brokerage.

(There are probably some extremely wealthy people who couldn't care less that their return on investment has been cut by 25 percent. But I don't know any of these folks, do you?)

Nonetheless, telemarketers need to *probe* to get the prospect to say this 25 percent change is a difference that makes a difference.

Once the investor says it's meaningful, she has unleashed an inner motivation to solve her problem. By this point, she has heard herself say:

- My current investment practices aren't giving me what they used to give me.

- In fact, they're seriously faltering, and I'm concerned about it.

All that's left to say is, "Dear broker, help me out!"

It's no coincidence that at this point in the conversation the seller asks, in effect: "Would you like my help?"

You can probably sense how a well-executed probing portion of a sales conversation can accomplish a great deal quickly. But I'd like to address an important issue that dramatizes the difference between traditional and the New Telemarketing: What if the prospect doesn't express an unmet need? If you can't evoke an unmet need from the prospect, you should bring the conversation to a swift but gracious conclusion. It's over. No pressure, no haranguing, no pestering. Conclude the call with the words, "Well, thank you for your courtesy!"

The New Telemarketing strategy doesn't force a product or service on an unwilling buyer. It's not only unethical, it's stupid! There are plenty of prospects in the universe who have real needs that they would love sellers' help in satisfying. In the same amount of time that it takes to hassle with a reluctant buyer, a salesperson can find a willing one.

By the same token, sellers want to end the call in these situations:

- You've uncovered an unmet need, but the prospect doesn't think it's important to her.

- You've uncovered an unmet need, and it's important, but the prospect doesn't want your help in addressing it.

As a consultant, I can tell you that I've run into plenty of prospects who sounded needy and were qualified to buy but didn't want outside help. Please remember this: An unmet need, alone, doesn't give you a motivated prospect.

EXAMPLE 2: PROBING

Probing is so important that I'm going to give you another tour through this procedure.

One of my clients sells a nifty scholarship and loan information service to parents of seniors in high school.

After announcing who the caller is, the company name, and a credibility statement, my client's probing segment of the conversation goes like this:

Seller:	Where is Mary thinking of attending college?
Customer:	Loyola Marymount.
Seller:	That's a fine school. Approximately how much do you think it's going to cost each year?
Customer:	I don't want to think about it!
Seller:	I understand, but what's your rough guess?
Customer:	About $20,000 per year.
Seller:	Including room and board?
Customer:	Nope. She's commuting!
Seller:	That's quite a large investment to make, isn't it?
Customer:	You can say that again!
Seller:	If I could show you some sources of loans, grants, and scholarships that Mary might qualify for, would that ease the burden a little?
Customer:	It sure would. What do you have?

Let's review the probing sequence to make sure I followed the steps:

1. What was my circumstances question? Right: "Where is Mary thinking of attending college?" It's a good question because it can elicit some friendly conversation while leading comfortably to the next step.

2. What was the unmet-need question? You won a new Chevy if you said, "Approximately how much do you think that's going to cost each year?"

A good way to identify an unmet-need question is to see whether it passes the "Ouch!" test. If it gets a prospect to nearly yelp, it is a good one. Did this one pass the test? How about the one from the first example?

3. Of course, our significance question is: "That's quite a large investment to make, isn't it?" Again, this is a reality test on the importance of the unmet need to that specific person.

The seller of this service will inevitably find people who will say: "It is, but we've been saving for her college education since she was born, so it's really to be expected."

How should the seller respond to this comment? Well, that's delightful. Have a great day. Good-bye!

That's right, it's a good time to pack up and to find someone who needs the financial help. There are plenty of such parents.

4. Our finale, of course, is the "If-then" question that probes for the prospect's desire for help.

Refining The Prober's Art

Your question-asking ability and the quality of the responses you elicit will definitely improve with practice. To help you to develop this skill, it's important for me to share with you the *four forms* of questions that you can use.

They are (1) open, (2) narrow, (3) closed, and (4) leading. They should actually appear this way on the page because it's often desirable to use them in sequence:

OPEN

NARROW

CLOSED

LEADING

Each form of question is valuable in itself because it will determine the amount and value of information that a prospect will give you. But, when you put them together in the proper sequence, you'll find they can get the most tight-lipped prospect to babble on like a bubbling brook.

Let's examine each question, in order.

Open Questions

Open questions cast a wide net in order to promote a freely flowing conversation. They enable prospects to open up and to divulge information in whatever quantity they wish.

Circumstances and unmet-needs questions are usually "open."

Let's draw from the two examples I gave you earlier to see how open questions work.

- "What kinds of investments are you attracted to now?"

- "Where is Mary thinking of attending college?"

You'll notice that these probes enable prospects to customize their answers to suit themselves. This gives them a feeling of freedom, and it avoids the feeling that you're trying to trap them into answering a specific way.

Narrow Questions

Narrow questions call for more specific answers. Here are two examples:

- "How are today's lower interest rates affecting the performance of those investments?"

- "Approximately how much do you think that's going to cost you each year?"

Both these questions should elicit numbers or dollar figures, or their equivalents. This form of question enables buyers to quantify their own unmet needs.

Closed Questions

Closed questions ask for a yes or a no. Examples:

- "If I could show you some ways to get a higher return on your investments without sacrificing safety, would you like to explore them further?"

- "If we could show you some sources of loans, grants, and scholarships that Mary might qualify for, would that ease the burden a little?"

If you want a specific, short answer, the closed question is the type to use.

Leading Questions

As you might have guessed, the leading question is really a statement that is made in the form of a question. It is structured the same way as the assumptive-checkback close, which I discussed earlier in this chapter. Here's an example: "That's quite a large investment to make, isn't it?"

The leading question can be the most insistent of the four types. It almost forces a prospect to concede a point, or to agree. But it has its place, even in the New Telemarketing, as you'll see.

Probing the Reluctant Prospect

What if you are trying to sell to a shy person or to someone who isn't immediately forthcoming with answers that you can use to build your sales conversation?

That's when you need to use the T-funnel. Imagine a funnel. At the top is an open question. A quarter of the way down the funnel is the narrow question. Another quarter of the way down is the closed question. Finally, at the bottom is the leading question. That's the T-funnel, because it looks like the letter T. Here's how it would look:

O P E N

N A R R O W

C L O S E D

LEADING

I'm going to revisit Example 1, but this time, I'm going to make the prospect much less forthcoming. Please observe that I ask different types of questions as I move down the funnel, to get the prospect to disclose an unmet need.

Example One Revisited

Broker:	What kinds of investments are you attracted to now?
Investor:	The same as I've always had.
Broker:	What types are they? Savings, T-bills, bonds?
Investor:	I have my money in CDs and municipal bonds, mostly.
Broker:	Savings accounts, too?
Investor:	Yes.
Broker:	How are today's lower interest rates affecting the performance of those investments?
Investor:	What do you mean?
Broker:	Are you earning less interest on your investments today vs. five or six years ago?
Investor:	I might be.
Broker:	What was the highest rate you were paid on a CD?
Investor:	I got 15 percent, once!
Broker:	And now?
Investor:	What am I getting now?
Broker:	Right.
Investor:	Now, I'm lucky to get 6 percent.
Broker:	So your return has dropped by 65 percent or more?

Investor:	If you say so.
Broker:	Does that bother you?
Investor:	Sure.
Broker:	How has it affected your lifestyle?
Investor:	What do you mean?
Broker:	Are you having to be more careful with your spending because you aren't seeing those big interest rates?
Investor:	I suppose so.
Broker:	If I could show you some simple ways to get a higher return on your investments without sacrificing safety, would you like to look into them?
Broker:	I'm listening. What interest rate are you paying?

I had fun writing this revised example. Reluctant prospects sound like characters from the old "Dragnet" TV shows, don't they?

When my open questions didn't work, what sorts of questions did I turn to? I went down the funnel, sometimes in order.

For instance, when the prospect balked after I asked her the circumstances question about her current investments, I rephrased it into a narrow question.

I gave her various options to select: "What types are they? Savings, T-bills, bonds?" Sometimes, you'll need to offer prompts such as these.

My next open probe was about lower interest rates. This time, my inquiry was rebuffed with a typical bounce-back: "What do you mean?"

I selected a closed probe, to cut to the chase: "Are you earning less interest on your investments today vs. five or six years ago?"

If I had trouble extracting quality information at this point, I would have packed my briefcase, or I could have used a leading question: "You can't be as happy now, with today's puny interest rates, when compared to the double-digit rates of years gone by, right?"

If a leading question doesn't hit the mark at this point, call the coroner — your prospect doesn't have a pulse!

At times, you may feel you're being asked to spoon-feed questions to your prospects. Be patient with them. It could be that they're not used to communicating in detail about what you're trying to sell.

In the previous dialogue I had to convert a narrow question into a closed type in this exchange: "How has it affected your lifestyle?"

"What do you mean?"

"Are you having to be more careful with your spending because you aren't seeing those big interest rates?"

Probing: Some Final Words

To sum up, I hope you'll see that probing is critical to the impact of the New Telemarketing.

These questions involve the customer. They encourage listeners to open up and to disclose quality information to you, the seller. Probing also gets them to say that (1) They have a need; (2) it's important; and (3) they want your help to solve it.

We have also discussed the four forms of questions, which you can use to get prospects to become motivated to buy. These are open, narrow, closed, and leading questions.

Now that you understand how to probe, we need to look at the remaining parts of the anatomy of a conversational sale. These components include the discussion, focusing, and commitment steps.

THE DISCUSSION

The discussion segment of the conversational sale is fairly straightforward. Its purpose is to provide customers with various options for solving their problems.

In the investment example, the seller could have followed his probing with a description of two or three of the investments with which the investor is familiar that could provide an above-average return with low risk.

In our college financing example, the sales rep could have discussed a few sources of loans or grants that might be available, yet still be unknown to the parent.

The New Telemarketing tries to offer more than one solution whenever possible. This gives buyers the comfort of knowing they have choices that can help to address their unmet needs.

It also helps the seller to avoid seeming like a person who is pitching a one-size-fits-all solution to everybody. If telmarketers come across that way, they can lose a lot of credibility.

Once you have discussed various potential solutions, you can introduce a step that is very specific to the conversational school of selling: The Focusing Step.

FOCUSING

When telemarketers have discussed potential solutions, it is very appropriate to ask the prospect: "At this point, which of these options would you like to look into further?"

This question puts buyers into the driver's seat. They tell you what is attractive to them, and what isn't.

If there is a solution that buyers simply don't want to pursue, they'll probably steer you away from it. This is great, because it will save you time.

COMMITMENT

Engineering commitment is essential to any kind of persuasion. In the conversational selling process, commitment occurs gradually, throughout the conversation. As customers respond to questions, they are discovering their needs while voicing their motivation to address them.

By the time you have walked them through various options in the discussion stage, prospects are ready to consider specific remedies. Asking them to focus on a most attractive remedy secures their commitment even further.

Commitments can vary in magnitude. You might obtain an outright commitment to buy, in which at the end of the call, the customer gives you a purchase order or charge-card number.

Or, you could get a prospect to agree to review your sales literature or to receive a fax. A commitment could also occur when you have been granted an appointment.

Many insurance and real estate executives, among others, work on an appointment basis. They'll put together a three-part marketing procedure:

1. They'll phone prospects to qualify their interest and capability to buy. Providing the sellers have been given green lights by the buyers, the sellers will ask for an appointment.

2. The next step is to visit the prospects and to put together a proposal.

3. The third step is to call or to visit the prospects to obtain their final approval of the deal.

Throughout this sequence, the sellers are trying to move the buyers through increasing levels of commitment. It can take many interactions before a proposal is approved.

In the New Telemarketing, sellers act like consultants. This is why you'll sometimes see this form of selling referred to as "consultative." Consultants need to uncover needs and devise a plan for satisfying them that will be profitable to both consultants and clients. This is exactly what the New Telemarketer does.

It could take consultants several appointments with various "influencers" in a firm to engineer enough support to launch a new project. For instance, I'm at work right now with a firm that I would like to have as a client.

So far, I have communicated by letter to the CEO. He gave my materials to the VP/chief financial officer. I spoke to him and set an appointment to visit one of the firm's large service centers.

During my visit, I met with the VP/CFO and his site manager. Through that process, I identified two needs. I faxed a letter describing the needs to the CFO. Within the letter, I requested permission to visit a regional site.

I met with the same site manager I had met with before at the service center. We had a detailed discussion. I then observed some of the work flow, and I met with a regional manager. That meeting yielded another important need.

So far, I haven't submitted a proposal. It's possible that I'll invest in having two more meetings before I propose anything.

Why does it take so long? And aren't these preliminaries awfully expensive?

In some organizations, you'll find you need to meet all the key players and promote a certain amount of consensus before your proposal will have a chance of being approved.

Of course, it is expensive (in a sense) to invest in so many preliminary activities without knowing that a sale will be made. I am out of pocket for everything I do before a contract is made.

But this is simply a cost of doing business in the marketplace I have chosen. It takes time to get to know prospects, to think like them, and to see how I can be of the greatest service.

Moreover, my alternatives are worse. If I don't invest the time to get to know my prospects and their specific needs, I'll be writing proposals that are so vague that they'll fail. Any time I will have invested through the proposal stage will have been completely wasted.

Professional selling requires a certain amount of wisdom. You need to develop a sixth sense for which prospects are worth your time. Once you have found one who qualifies, you need to be patient.

Like a tiny sprout, it needs frequent watering and an environment that supports its growth. Then it can be harvested. If you try to rush the process, you'll throw it into shock. And you'll be faced with one dead prospect.

In this chapter, we've examined two ways to handle the outbound telemarketing call: using traditional and New Telemarketing methods. In the next chapter, we'll turn our attention to mastering the inbound telemarketing call.

Chapter Five

Mastering the Inbound Call

Some people get agitated when they hear a telephone ring. Not me. I light up because I hear the sweet sound of opportunity. Inbound calls can offer treasure or tribulations depending on how we manage them.

For example, just yesterday I phoned a university to enlist it in sponsoring one of my Six-Figure Consulting seminars. The person who answered the phone in the Continuing Education Division seemed to have a dire case of heartburn.

I announced who I was and asked who was in charge of professional development programs. The receptionist blurted out a name so fast, and with such negativity, that I needed to check to determine whether I had heard it correctly.

"Yeah, that's it," she shot back, stopping abruptly. I was forced to nudge the conversation along. "May I speak to her, please?"

Silence. Then a long pause, and then the extension rang. Pleasantly, the person I was connected to was a complete contrast to the secretary. She was upbeat, warm, and human.

And I felt better about the possibility of creating an alliance with her school. But I'm still concerned that if my registrants call and wind up speaking to Witch Hazel, they're going to be turned off and change their minds. And all our hard work invested in advertising and in public relations to get potential registrants to call will rapidly go down the drain.

This chapter is designed to help you to avoid ugly outcomes like this and to make the most you possibly can of the calls that come your way. Let me set the tone for what is going to follow in the course of the next several pages.

I should point something out that I consider very important. In my way of thinking, there is no such thing as a pure "sales" or a pure "service" call. *All* customer contacts by telephone have sales and service impacts. Smart people and smart companies optimize both outcomes in as many calls as they possibly can.

When we study the underpinnings of communication, we learn that the differences between providing information and persuading someone are exaggerated.

Let's say someone calls your company and asks for literature. You agree to send it, and the call is terminated at that point.

What kind of a call has that been: informative or persuasive? During the contact you indicated information was available and you informed the person that you'd be mailing it or faxing it. The caller knew that she learned something. So in large measure, the call was informative in nature.

But how you treated that person during the call, and how credible and capable you sounded, will have a big-time persuasive impact as well. You'll predispose the person to either look forward to doing business with you or want to avoid it. So when this person receives your literature, he or she is going to feel either more or less inclined to act on it, depending how telephonically effective you were.

WHO CONTROLS THE CALL?

One of my goals for this chapter is to show you how to make even elementary telephone encounters sparkle. And it can be done through the proper use of three critical elements: *text, tone*, and *timing*.

But there is another false assumption that I want to discuss before we get into the mechanics of handling inbound "opportunities." That is the belief that if clients or prospects call us, it is "their call," but if we call them, it is "our call."

This belief leads us to be *passive* communicators if we received the calls but *active* communicators if we initiated them.

I hope you're smiling right now as you read this, because I am. What a foolish thought, right?

Where is it written, in the Great Book of Business, that the initiator of the contact has an immutable right to control the flow of the call?

How absurd, right? Yet, many people seem to buy into this; therefore, they allow calls to become wandering, inefficient, and random encounters. For instance, I've heard countless customer service reps declare: "The customer was already mad when he called, and I couldn't do anything about it!"

Nice try, but that dog won't hunt. Certainly, some customers arrive in our ears, "uncorked," but we should be savvy enough to get these menacing genies back into the bottle willingly and happily. To say, in so many words, that we can't control telephone outcomes is simply a lot of bunk.

Here's another gem that I come across: "He was in a hurry, so I didn't have time to tell him about our specials!"

We should be the ones who set the pace of calls, not the customer. When we do a proper job of timing management, customers will follow our lead and slow down. In just a moment, I'll provide you with a pivotal statement that will induce customers to gratefully give you control of their calls.

There is a key similarity in the two quotes that I've attacked. It is this belief: We're not in control of inbound calls — customers are.

If you endorse that idea, I promise you it will come true. To get the most you can from this chapter, you'll need to reverse that statement. You should start telling yourself, right now, before you read another word of this section, that: "I'm the master of inbound calls, and, can determine how much productivity I glean from them."

There is a significant reason I encourage you to switch concepts. It's something that I've found time and again: Left to their own devices, customers won't produce optimal call outcomes for us or for themselves.

Let me explain what I mean. Unlike you, customers aren't trained communicators. They don't know how to manage telephone contacts so they're brief but thoroughly productive. For instance, they feel they have to overtalk to explain preliminaries in detail before telemarketers can help them.

Yet, if telemarketers aren't armed with friendly countermeasures to keep customers from rambling, they'll go on forever, and sellers will have stacks of calls on hold to wrestle with when blabbers finally get off the line.

Furthermore, customers haven't been trained to make calls end on a positive, emotional note. So if sellers give over control of calls to them, customers will tonally "trough," as they conclude, so everyone will sound negative instead of positive.

By taking responsibility for the inbound call and by using some of the vocal techniques I'm going to share with you, you'll make calls end so happily that customers will get hooked on those feelings and they'll come back for more.

But to make that happen, sellers need to transform the inbound call process from a random occurrence into a planned system — a system that uses scripts, or what I refer to as "call paths."

THE INBOUND NEW TELEMARKETING APPROACH

If inbound calls should be treated like outbound calls, it is only logical to recycle what you already know about outbound calls.

You'll recall from our last chapter that the outbound call has several components:

OPENER

PROBING

DISCUSSION

FOCUSING

COMMITMENT

The inbound anatomy of a telemarketing call is strikingly similar to the outbound version. It has an opener, but salespeople don't supply it — the customer does. She might say, "I saw your ad in the newspaper, and I wanted some more information."

In this sense, she's doing the inbound equivalent of our "after-advertising" opener. The big mistake we make is by skipping down to our discussion section. Usually, we'll just start blabbing about the product she mentioned.

What I'm going to suggest is that you use a very powerful line that I've devised. You started the call with: "Hello, Goodman Communications, this is Sara. How may I help you?"

That's a very conventional and appropriate greeting for an inbound call. Then, the customer says: "I saw your ad in the newspaper, and I wanted some more information."

I urge you to respond with these precise words: "Sure, I'll be happy to help you with that!"

What purpose does this response serve? Well, there are several. Let's start our explanation by noting how customers *feel* when they call a company for service or to buy something.

Typically, (1) they're afraid they won't get the help or the service they want; and (2) they're concerned that even if they receive help, it will require that they work hard to get it. In other words, it won't be an enjoyable transaction.

Another way of putting this is to say that customers are usually uptight when they call. And they'll stay that way, and therefore be less subject to a seller's persuasion, until the seller does something proactive, and immediate, to change their feelings.

That's where the "promise of help" line comes to the rescue. By saying, "Sure, I'll be happy to help you with that!" this pledge says: "Rest assured that you'll get what you're looking for, and I'm going to enjoy providing it to you."

That, my friend, is a power-packed message to send to someone at the beginning of a call. Here's what will happen when you use it.

People will relax. They'll literally breathe a sigh of relief. You'll hear them exhale, and if you don't, many will explicitly respond at that point and say: "Oh, great!"

You will have accomplished something exceedingly powerful at the beginning of the conversation. You will have injected an early customer satisfaction into the call. It'll create rapport, and callers will do a few other helpful things for you.

They'll usually give you control of the conversation. This is significant because you can use this control to advance to the next portion of the anatomy of an inbound call: the probing section.

You'll find that if you don't have a promise of help people will be quite impatient with your probes, because they'll wonder how your questions are connecting with their purpose for calling. With a promise of help, they'll know you're committed to giving them what they want, so they'll perceive your questions as being pertinent to them. They'll relax and be more patient with you. This will reduce tension for you and for your customer!

Let me give you an incredible example. I don't know any companies that wouldn't love to have their customer service and telemarketing reps "up-sell" and "suggestively sell" customers. This is when people call to buy product *A*, and the seller also persuades them to buy *B*, or persuades them to buy more of *A* than the customers had anticipated buying.

One of my software clients sent out mailers for a $30 product upgrade. Customers called in to order it, but telemarketers were asked to up-sell them to a $99 "bonus bundle," instead. When sellers didn't have the promise of help, callers resented the attempt to "switch them" from the cheaper offer, *A*, to the more expensive offer, *B*.

After I was retained to redesign the conversations and sellers inserted the promise of help, there were zero complaints. How come? Customers were assured from the get-go that they were going to receive what they wanted. Knowing this, they allowed the rep to move on with the call.

As it turned out, this opening sequence led nicely to the probing section, for which I had prepared a single, Perfect Question for sellers to use. Here it is:

> Did you just want the conventional upgrade, or are you interested in the Special Bonus Bundle?

This seems like a simple clarifying question, but it was unusually potent. It told the customer that there was a better package to buy without foisting it on them.

Notice the language here. Did callers "just want the conventional upgrade?" That sounds dull, doesn't it? Who wants to be conventional?

"Or are you interested in the Special Bonus Bundle?" Now, that sounds exciting, doesn't it? In light of the fact that callers didn't read anything about the Bonus Bundle, they were intrigued — so intrigued that most prospects asked to be sold!

Specifically, they commanded, "Tell me about the bonus!"

You can guess what followed, can't you? The next step of the anatomy of an inbound call, of course: the discussion.

At this point, sellers could take their time to describe the bonus bundle. Because it was a single purchase-item, they didn't need the focusing step, so they simply advanced to the commitment step.

And, I realize this is hard to believe, but I have tape recordings to prove it:

Customers, more often than not, *closed themselves before sellers could do it!*

They'd hear the description, and as the rep was transitioning into the commitment stage, customers would take the sale away from them, and say: "Send me the bonus!"

So, let's review what happened in this inbound call:

1. The opener was provided by the customer.

2. The seller inserted a promise of help.

3. The seller probed with a Perfect Question.

4. The customer asked for a description, which the rep provided.

5. The customer committed voluntarily, or the seller used commitment phraseology.

Here is the basic outline of the Anatomy of an Inbound Call:

OPENER
(customer provides it)

PROMISE OF HELP

PROBING

DISCUSSION

FOCUSING
(if there are multiple products that were described)

COMMITMENT

As you can see, it is 80 percent to 90 percent similar to the anatomy of an outbound call, as it should be.

LET'S MERGE SERVICE AND SALES CALLS, SHALL WE?

There are customer service departments that don't sell; however, they're becoming increasingly rare. Many of those that do sell aren't very effective because they haven't figured out a way of blending sales and service call paths.

For instance, a call will come into a customer service or a technical support department and the caller will ask a question. The technician will answer it, and then, at the very end of the call he will paste on a segment that sounds like this:

> Have you heard about our Jiffy Bag special? Right now, they're two-for-the-price-of-one. Would you like to order a dozen and get a dozen free?

This sort of "sales graft" doesn't work very well because it seems out of character with what has gone before in the conversation. In this section, I'm going to show you how to blend sales and service objectives in a single call.

To dramatize how viable this sales strategy is, I'd like to share with you information about how I helped one of my consulting clients to sell products to angry customers.

A number of years ago a famous camera manufacturer asked me to develop a special customer service sales program. My mission was to teach customer service people to sell new products to angry customers.

(In high school you may have been asked to study Marc Antony's famous funeral oration for the slain Julius Caesar. It was a tricky speech, because he had to transform an angry crowd into allies. Of course, he pulled it off beautifully, and that's why the speech is considered a classic. Selling to angry people requires the same sort of careful crafting.)

Imagine this scenario: A customer has purchased a camera, and it isn't working as it should. The customer calls an "800" number and is informed that the device must be sent to a repair center, and she won't get it back for up to six weeks.

Well, if the holidays are around the corner, Mrs. Jones doesn't want to be told she won't be able to memorialize the festive occasion through photographs. In a word, she'll be quite disappointed and, probably, angry.

My goal was to develop a call path and a suitable training program that would enable a customer service rep to assuage angry callers and sell them something new during the same telephone call. How can you emotionally elevate people from "down in the dumps" to a point of confidence where they'll feel good about buying something new? And how do you do this before their camera is even sent into the shop and before it has been fixed?

It would seem next-to-impossible, right? It isn't.

It *does* require new thinking: (1) Salespeople have to believe it is possible; and (2) they have to work out the theory and the mechanics of a process that will take the possible and turn it into real, everyday communication practices.

In the case of the camera manufacturer, it is to the company's credit that it had managers who were thinking creatively. They saw that their customer service unit was an expensive cost center, fielding thousands of calls every day that didn't result in immediate sales.

So management wanted a way to get the toll-free calls to pay their own way. They found me, and I was prepared, intellectually and experientially, to think through the method for performing the task.

It should be said, of course, that the camera company didn't, under any circumstances, want to seem crass or insensitive when selling. I couldn't have implemented a call script that went like this:

Customer:	"Hello, my camera broke while I was trying to load the film. Where can I get it fixed?"
Rep:	"I'll tell you about that in a minute, but first, let's talk about this special we have on photo albums!"

No, that wouldn't have worked. The company needed to earn the right to sell something new, and here is the five-step process I invented:

1. Resolve the conflict with a smile; instruct the customer how to send the camera in, and so on.

2. Apologize at least twice — once upon hearing the problem and again after "solving" the problem;

3. Resell the customer on the wisdom of her original decision to purchase that particular camera. Then, when she agrees it was a desirable product to own,

4. tell her that there's something nice that goes along with it, that happens to be on "special" — a carrying case, a flash attachment, or a photo album.

5. Whether she buys the new item or not, thank her, sincerely, for doing business with your company.

What were the results of the program? It worked — big time. Customers felt they were being treated well and that their problems were being pleasantly addressed.

They didn't feel they were "being sold," which is critical. And the company found that customers were much more committed to the camera and to the company because they were encouraged to become resold on the wisdom of their original purchase.

So the great concern that customers would become alienated by being sold never became an actuality. Pleasantly, the opposite occurred: customers identified even more strongly with the manufacturer.

THREE NEW GOALS FOR SERVICE AND SALES CALLS

It's one thing to make a sale or to answer a customer's inquiry politely. But telemarketers can make calls accomplish much more than this.

Specifically, when sellers manage calls effectively, they can: (1) Get customers to thank them profusely, (2) get customers to "sing," and (3) get customers to recommit their business and express their loyalty to the firm.

Wow, that's a lot to ask from a phone call, isn't it? Not really. Let me share with you some breakthroughs that I helped a mutual fund client to achieve in its customer service program.

This company employed about 200 people in the service area. To give you an idea as to why I was called in as a consultant, let's look at its sorry record, to that point. According to its own surveys, the customer service department had the lowest employee satisfaction rankings of any unit.

As you might imagine, its clients didn't like the treatment they received at the hands of these unhappy folks. According to an independent firm, the company ranked number 24 out of 26 in customer satisfaction for companies surveyed in its industry.

In a word, its customer service wasn't good. But the company did have new management, and these leaders were very capable. They realized they had an opportunity to create a best-in-class service department, so I was given carte blanche to rebuild the unit's work processes.

Here's what I did. I listened closely to phone conversations. After all, every call wasn't poor in quality, and some were outstanding. No one had figured out what the recipe was for producing exceptional customer outcomes, call after call.

That was my mandate. I determined that customers were capable of doing the three things I mentioned above: they could express gratitude, sing, and recommit — if they were treated exceptionally well.

In studying calls, I figured out that there were certain times when customers did these things spontaneously. I examined closely the treatment they had received before engaging in these fireworks.

And then, I set forth to create a call path that would encourage customers to do these things, call after call — even if they simply called for a price quotation on a mutual fund.

Now, the call path has been in operation for about seven years, and after about 10 million calls, here's what has happened:

- Employee satisfaction soared so much that customer service was rated the number one unit in the firm in terms of employee satisfaction.

- Employee turnover, which had been about 100 percent per year, dropped below 10 percent, which is a normal and acceptable attrition level.

- The same outside agency that ranked the department 24 out of 26 participating firms awarded six consecutive first-place awards to the unit.

- The department was written up in *The Wall Street Journal* as one of "The Best in Service" in its industry.

- Phone calls got shorter and better. This saved the company millions of dollars.

So, as the president of the firm put it, they "Went from worst to first," and they have stayed there, year after year.

THE CRITICAL CYCLE OF COMMITMENT AND RECOMMITMENT

The only place that service and sales departments really exist as neatly separate entities is on organizational charts. These distinctions aren't commonplace in the minds of customers, however.

The mutual fund company experience demonstrated that the chief aim of customer service isn't to provide information, though that is one of the things such a unit does. But information isn't its highest vocation.

The key to brilliant service and service that sells is getting customers to recommit their business, and this requires both persuasion and a real investment of focused effort. A sales department, in this way of thinking, might be chiefly concerned with engineering customer commitment.

Imagine the recycling symbol that appears on so many plastic bottles. It shows arrows flowing in an unbroken circle. This is the image I have in mind when I characterize the commitment – recommitment cycle that is involved in handling inbound calls.

Sometimes a service department — as in the case of the camera manufacturer — can transform anger into recommitment, then the recommitment into a new commitment or a new sale, all in a single, seamless transaction.

HOW TO TRANSFORM ANGER INTO RECOMMITMENT

Let's look at the units that would be involved in transforming an angry call into a new sale. The initial steps are identical to those found in handling a "pure" inbound sales call, except service-/salespeople are aiming at recommitment, not a sales commitment:

OPENER
(customer provides it and states problem)

PROMISE OF HELP

PROBING
(to determine exactly the nature of the problem — its history, etc.)

DISCUSSION
(offers possible solutions to problem)

FOCUSING
(on most suitable solution to the customer)

RECOMMITMENT
(resells customer on desirability of original purchase)

Once a recommitment has been made, the call ends, and the customer is happy. The problem is solved and the caller feels good about the rep, the product, and the company.

But service-/salespeople don't have to stop there. They can shift into a sales mode by attaching three of the steps from the anatomy of an inbound call. Here's what we should add:

PROBING II
(to determine unmet needs)

DISCUSSION II
(to offer a new product or service to meet those needs)

COMMITMENT
(to get the customer to purchase the new item)

I need to point out a few really important dynamics that should assuage your concerns that a call of this type could seem unusual or cumbersome:

- Appreciate that there are several mood shifts that occur that will earn you the right to evolve from a service to a sales mode. Remember that you'll use a promise of help that will calm customers and deliver an early sense of satisfaction.

- You'll fully listen to the customer's problem while offering one or more potential solutions.

- You'll discuss the desirability of the original purchase with the customer, so she'll be thinking, "If I had to do it over, I'd buy this again!"

Thus, callers wind up in a good mood and want to reward you. The way they'll do it is by conversing with you further and perhaps buying your add-on product.

The next page shows the full sequence in a handy, easy-to-read and remember format.

So, here is the full rendering of the service-into-sales call:

OPENER
(customer provides it and states problem)

PROMISE OF HELP

PROBING
(to determine exactly the nature of the problem —
its history, etc.)

DISCUSSION
(offers possible solutions to problem)

FOCUSING
(on most suitable solution to the customer)

RECOMMITMENT
(resells customer on desirability of original purchase)

PROBING II
(to determine unmet needs)

DISCUSSION II
(to offer a new product or service to meet those needs)

NEW COMMITMENT
(to get the customer to purchase the new item)

REMEMBER YOUR INBOUND CALL-HANDLING ETIQUETTE

There are several additional procedures to employ to ensure that your calls produce the service and sales results.

Make sure to sharpen these basic telephone communication skills:

- Make sure to *articulate*. Fully form your words so they are completely comprehensible to your listeners. Many of your customers will have a degree of hearing loss. If a seller sounds mumble-mouthed during the call, prospects will miss what the seller is saying and grow frustrated. No one wants to buy when he or she is in a foul mood.

- Put a *smile* into your speech. How can you sound cheerful? When you come to the ends of sentences, make sure to lift a few up, tonally, instead of allowing your tone to continuously decline. It'll give you and your customer a lift!

- Adopt the proper *speed* for speaking. Most Americans speak at a rate of 100 – 150 words per minute. If you speak far beyond this range, you'll probably annoy your listener.

- *Take turns* speaking and listening. It can be upsetting when callers feel that people are speaking when the callers haven't stopped speaking.

- Say *please* and *thank-you* with great frequency. People never tire of sincerely expressed politeness.

- Don't overuse the *hold button*. If you have to place someone on hold, ask if it's okay to do so: "May I ask you to hold?"

  Then predict and tell customers how long they'll be in that state of suspended animation: "It should only take me about 30 seconds and I'll be back, okay?"

- *Always call back* when you've promised to do so. If you say, "I'll call you back with that information by 4," then do so, even if you don't have the information you thought you'd have.

- *Answer your voice-mail and e-mail messages promptly.* A speedy response is almost always appreciated in sales and service situations.

- *Thank customers* for their patience if they have been waiting on hold before reaching you.

- Remember that *each call is like a performance.* When the curtain goes up and you're connected to a customer, it's "Show time!" Don't let customers down by sounding less than completely enthusiastic.

TAKE YOUR CALLS TO THE NEXT LEVEL

Productivity is often defined as getting a high degree of output from input.

When you take an inbound call, it contains numerous opportunities that go far beyond the ordinary. Don't be bashful about exploiting as many of these as you can.

For example, I called the printer of my seminar brochures to tell him that I'd be cutting back on my mailings. I wanted to give him timely notice so he could schedule his staff accordingly.

Many people, on hearing this, would have said, "Fine, thanks for telling me, Gary." And that would have been that.

But my printer went beyond that. He said, "Gee, I'm sorry to hear that. How come you're cutting back?"

Can you see how he was using a call path not unlike the one that I've given you? What was he doing? He was probing, right?

Well, I told him that I wasn't happy with my direct mailing results, so I was exploring other marketing channels, such as publicity and magazine advertising.

He wouldn't make money if I did that, so he set forth to try to cure my underlying problem so I could continue giving him large brochure orders. He said: "I'd like to have a direct mail consultant call you. Maybe he could help you improve your results."

I have to admire my printer for his effort. Not only might that have solved my problem, had I taken him up on it, but he would no doubt have earned a finder's fee from the consultant, as well.

The printer was fully alert to the *opportunities* that my "downer" of a call offered, and he wasn't afraid to exploit them. Good for him!

Please think of my printer the next time your telephone rings. You could transform lemons into lemonade just as he was doing and in the same manner that the camera manufacturer did. It requires only that you alter your perception about what is achievable while implementing call paths that will help you to reach your objectives.

In the next chapter, we'll explore why conventional "objections" tend to disappear when you employ the New Telemarketing. But just in case they don't, I'll provide you with some surefire ways of conquering them, whether the objections arise in the beginning, the middle, or at the end of your calls.

CHAPTER SIX

WHAT HAPPENED TO ALL OF THE OBJECTIONS?

Even the most experienced salespeople on Earth aren't pleased about having to handle objections, but doing so is part of the job. First of all, what is an objection?

An *objection* can be a simple interruption of your sales talk, or it can be a reason or excuse not to buy. Imagine calling someone. You introduce yourself, and the prospect says: "I'm busy right now."

That's an objection. It stops the flow of your ideas, and if it is left unaddressed, the conversation will end at that point.

Another very common objection you'll hear, especially at the beginning of the call, is: "I'm not interested."

How should telemarketers treat these interruptions? And is there a way of avoiding them altogether? We'll deal with these challenges in this chapter.

Just to give you some perspective on my experience with objections, I'll share a story with you. When I worked for Time/Life, early in my career, we cold-called people at home to sell the wonderful books that company continues to make.

Of course, if people weren't familiar with the terrific color photos the books contained or the fine value represented by Time/Life's low prices, they'd throw objections our way.

As a manager, I asked my reps to note every time they heard an objection. What we discovered was nothing less than amazing: 80 percent of our sales came after at least one objection was uttered and successfully rebutted.

Wow! This is meaningful because salespeople who were stopped cold by the first objection they heard denied themselves four sales for every one that they earned. In other words, they were "giving away" 80 percent of their potential sales by not successfully responding to interruptions!

So *answering* objections pays off!

If you employ a traditional form of telemarketing you can expect to hear lots of objections. Generally, if you use a more polite, needs-based form of telemarketing, you'll hear fewer objections. They'll also tend to occur earlier in conversations. I'll show you how to deal with objections no matter what telemarketing style you choose to use.

THE SIX STANDARD OBJECTIONS

There are several classical objections:

- No money — "I can't afford it."

- No value — "It costs too much."

- No interest — "I'm not interested."

- No need — "I don't need it."

- No time — "I can't talk right now."

- No authority to buy — "I'm not in charge."

First, let's discuss what customers are really saying when they throw out these interruptions. When someone says he or she can't afford something, it could be true or false.

I believe the best way to deal with this objection is to believe it, to say good-bye, and to go on to the next prospect. How come?

If someone has no money, he's unqualified to buy, so salespeople shouldn't annoy him or ourselves by persisting with the call. I'd simply end it by saying, "Well, thank you for your courtesy!"

Of course, there's an exception to this rule. If you are in the business of financing individual purchases through a credit plan or extended payments, then you can truly help the buyer and still make the sale.

If someone says something costs too much, he's telling you he isn't sold on its utility or value to him. I have a friend who told me, back in 1984, that the turbodiesel station wagon I bought cost way too much.

Well, it currently has 160,000 miles on it, and mechanics tell me the engine could make it to 500,000 miles if I treat it right. So my car, which cost twice as much as other wagons of its time, will probably endure five times longer.

If my friend had been a car buyer, and I was the salesperson, I would have had to explain something like what I just explained to you in order to dramatize the product's value.

My persuasive goal would have been to prove the opposite: that it was underpriced, given its anticipated useful life. That's how you rebut a value objection. You should make the most *extreme* counterargument you can.

Of course, you're not shouting or becoming unglued. You're super-calm, but your argumentative position is as strong as it can possibly be.

Another objection is: "It's too soon to buy!" If you wanted to make the strongest possible rebuttal, what would it be? At least two possibilities rush to mind:

- It can never be too soon!

- It's later than you think!

Please keep in mind the fact that you won't be using these exact words when you formulate your response. Your entire response may be:

> Well I appreciate that it may seem too soon, but these items are in limited supply, and they're going fast. So let's set one aside for you now, and I'm sure you'll be pleased. Okay?

I've moved through three distinct steps in this response, which I'll explain thoroughly in a few minutes. For now, I wanted to show you that there's a difference between the counterargument you're going to use and the precise wording of it.

Let's press on to examine the next objection: "I'm not interested." This can mean at least two things depending on when it's uttered during the call. If you hear it immediately after your opener, it's usually an excuse to leave the conversation.

Seller:	Hello, I'm Gary Goodman...
Prospect:	I'm not interested!

Imagine hearing such a rapid-fire objection. This actually happened to me, and I hadn't even mentioned the name of my company. How could the person be interested? Had she spent enough time with the call to even know what it was about?

Of course not. Because it was a bogus objection, I used a special transition phrase designed to counter this attack and enable me to continue the conversation. Here's the entire beginning of that conversation:

Gary:	Hello, I'm Gary Goodman...
Prospect:	I'm not interested!
Gary:	Well, I'd be surprised if you were at this point, but I'm calling with Time/Life Books, and the reason I'm calling is that recently we sent out some letters and brochures. I was wondering, do you recall seeing one by any chance?

It was great. Do you know what happened, right after I countered with "Well, I'd be surprised if you were at this point ... ?"

The prospect giggled. She was blown away by the fact that her earliest-of-all-possible objections was responded to quickly and diplomatically. Do you know what happened after her laughter?

Nothing at all. She respectfully listened to the remainder of my presentation, and she actually turned into a buyer!

This is the power of a transition phrase in action. It serves as a bridge that spans the gap created by a customer's objection back to the next part of your presentation. Here's what happens, in sequence:

1. You begin the presentation.

2. The prospect objects.

3. You use a transition phrase and then pick up exactly where you left off.

Used properly, a transition phrase will help you to surpass the early roadblocks that prospects put in your way. You'll often find, as in the case of the person who cut me off super-fast, that customers don't have any more barriers after the first one. So you'll frequently be allowed to continue without further interruptions.

Of course, a transition phrase isn't designed to fully answer an objection. If you hear a bogus, early interruption, you'll use the phrase without a rebuttal.

At the end of your presentation, you'll treat the same objection differently. If you have gone through your entire sales talk and then someone says,

"I'm not interested," you have to assume that you didn't appeal to the person's needs.

If sellers haven't aroused a sense of need, it's natural for someone to assert that he or she is not interested. When this happens, sellers use the 3-step process I alluded to, above:

1. We'll use a transition phrase.

2. We'll answer the objection.

3. We'll engineer commitment with a close line.

This isn't quite so easy with the "not interested" objection, because telemarketers don't have much to go on. So the second step will involve probing to uncover needs, or sellers can offer a restatement of what they believe the prospect's needs to be.

Here's how the conversation might go:

Seller:	So, let's move forward, and I know you'll be pleased, Okay?
Prospect:	No, I'm not interested.
Seller:	Well, I appreciate that, but you *would* like to save money on your income taxes, am I right?
Prospect:	Sure.
Seller:	Well, then, let's give my company's service a try, then see what you think. Okay?

You can see that the same objection is treated differently depending on when it occurs. If it comes right at the beginning of the call, sellers treat it briefly with a transition phrase, then return to where the discussion left off.

An important assumption is that by hearing more of the seller's prepared talk, prospects will become increasingly interested as the seller continues. So, many of these early objections will dissolve within a few seconds because they'll be addressed by the presentation.

If the same objection happens after sellers have completed the presentation, they'll use a complete three-part procedure to address it.

But please note that the fuller process *still* begins with a transition phrase, so by having a good one on the tip of your tongue, you'll be able to respond quickly, no matter where you are in your talk when objections occur.

When people say, "I don't need it," they're obviously saying the sellers haven't aroused a sense of need. So sellers are going to treat this objection the same way they handled the "not interested" assertion.

When customers say, "I can't talk right now," or that they're busy, telemarketers can do at least two different things:

- Sellers can believe them and say, "Okay, I'll call you later," and move on to the next prospect who does seem to have time to interact. Often, you'll sense whether someone is preoccupied by their distracted or disjointed communication style. If it's real, why fight it?

- The second approach is the direct opposite. Sellers may not believe the prospects. It could sound, to sellers, like an early "Not Interested" excuse to duck the call. If so, you can say: "Well, I appreciate that, so I'll make it brief ... ."

Sometimes, that's all prospects want to hear — that you won't talk their ears off. By the way, I wouldn't shrink your presentation after you say this, because it'll diminish your persuasiveness and listeners won't have a clue as to how long your call was intended to be.

If someone says he or she has to get someone else's approval to buy, you can do several things:

- Make sure the customer *personally* supports the process. You can do this by asking: "Well, if the decision were up to you, would you, personally support moving ahead?" If customers hesitate in replying, they are simply trying to dodge having to make a commitment. From that point, you can give up on him, or find out who his boss is, and then speak directly to her.

- You can ask to have the absent decision-maker join the conversation on a conference-call basis, where the three of you can coordinate your efforts in "real time." This approach enables you to communicate directly with authorities, to ensure that they hear information first hand, and it keeps you from "going over the head" of your initial contact.

- You can "deputize" your contact to try to sell the boss on your behalf. Sometimes going through an intermediary in this way is the only method you'll be allowed to use to make progress. If so, try to rehearse your "champion" so he or she has all the arguments for moving forward with your proposal. Additionally, try to make sure he or she knows the answers to the boss's probable objections.

OBJECTIONS AND "CONFLICT" ARE DIFFERENT, BUT THEY SHOULD BE HANDLED IN MUCH THE SAME WAY

Although it may seem that someone who says "I'm not interested" is angry or uptight with you, he or she usually isn't, and it's a big mistake to misinterpret objections this way. Customer service people are operating under a misconception if they believe that conflict is abnormal. It isn't. As long as customers feel disappointed, there will be conflict.

The good news is that the way I've taught you to manage objections is suitable for managing conflict, with a few modifications.

Imagine a customer calls you, and the first words she utters are: "I'm really angry with you people!"

What could you say? You'd probably want to use a transition phrase of some sort to acknowledge her concerns and to enable you to regain control of the call.

It wouldn't be the phrase I introduced before: "Well, I'd be surprised if you weren't at this point!" That would sound foolish.

But you could use this one, which I've crafted, specifically, for handling conflict: "Gee, I'm sorry to hear you say that. Let's see where we can go from here … ."

I've used this line and I can tell you, it'll stop a speeding train. How come it's so effective?

It works because it contains every known supportive communication element. Supportive elements reduce or avoid conflict, whereas defensive elements increase conflict.

By starting with the kid-like word, "Gee," sellers sound *spontaneous*. By using, "I'm sorry ...," they convey *empathy*. When they say, "To hear you say that," we're using description. And by saying "Let's see," they introduce a *problem-solving approach and equality* into the situation. When they offer to see "where we can go from here," they convey *flexibility* and the idea that there are several possible solutions to the problem.

Here are six messages that make customers uptight and angry. It is worth your effort to avoid using them:

- **Evaluation.** If we criticize our customers or seem to be evaluating them as people, they'll feel they're being attacked, and they'll defend their hurt egos by attacking us. For example, let's say a person takes his car to a mechanic, and he tells the mechanic that he tried to fix the car himself. The mechanic might snap: "You shouldn't have done that!"

  The *supportive alternative* to this statement could have been: "You can probably fix a lot of things yourself, but you may want to bring the electrical problems to me, first. Then, if I think you can do it yourself, I'll be happy to let you know, okay?"

  This is a *description* instead of an *evaluation*, and it is usually accepted by clients without a fuss.

- **Control.** Let's say the customer asked the mechanic how much time he'd need to fix the car, and the mechanic said: "There's no way to tell until I get under the hood."

  He might be telling the truth, but by saying it the way he did, he could arouse defensiveness by making the client feel the mechanic was retaining all control over the repair information.

  A supportive mechanic might say: "It looks to me like it could be one of three things." Then, he would explain what they are and how much time would be required to make a diagnosis and a repair under each circumstance.

By defining the three possible problems in an objective way, the mechanic seems to be *sharing control* of the repair with the customer.

- **Strategy.** When someone is acting strategic, he seems like he's deliberately trying to withhold information from the customer. I was watching a TV program about secret military bases when a reporter tried to get information from a sentry. All the sentry said, in response to every question, was, "You're on private property, and you'll have to leave now."

  In this case, the sentry was doing his duty, and strategically withholding information is part of his job. Unfortunately, many people in the private sector act just like the sentry, but they don't have to.

- **Neutrality.** When sellers seem uncaring or indifferent toward customers and their problems, they are acting neutrally. If a customer called and asked, "Who should I speak to about this?" we would sound neutral and defensive by replying: "I don't know — it's not my job!"

  Empathy is the right emotion to project. This tells the customer that sellers know what it feels like to be in his or her shoes. And by showing concern, sellers avoid conflicts. When telemarketers sell with empathy, they avoid objections because prospects feel sellers have their best interests at heart.

- **Superiority.** Know-it-alls make others feel defensive and inferior because they seem to be constantly elevating their own stature at the expense of the customer. If you sound superior as a salesperson, you'll deny yourself many sales.

  Instead, treat the customer as an equal. You might want to remember this line that I heard from an exceedingly successful consultant: "Nice and humble does it every time."

- **Certainty.** If you told customers you possessed an exclusive knowledge of the *truth*, you'd probably make them want to puncture your bubble by showing you that you're wrong.

> People who sound dogmatic and unyielding in their ideas
> bring out in other people the desire to make them look foolish.
> This can be avoided by sounding *flexible*.

None other than the great Benjamin Franklin, who was a skilled diplomat, attributed his smooth dealings with others to the ability to sound less-than-extreme in his language when expressing his opinions and ideas.

Instead of saying, "I know" something, he'd say, "I sense" that such-and-such is the case. This would win support for his ideas while making him seem like an exceedingly moderate person. For more information about his approach, read his timeless book, *The Autobiography of Benjamin Franklin*.

IF YOUR TELEMARKETING IS POLITE AND CONVERSATIONAL, OBJECTIONS WILL BE MORE POLITE AND LESS FREQUENT

My clients have found that when they use the New Telemarketing, they have a vastly different experience with objections than people who employ traditional telemarketing.

Because New Telemarketing seeks to establish client needs at the beginning of a call, this shifts the relationship from being defensive and adversarial to supportive and mutual. When clients feel you are trying to address their specific situation, they are less likely to throw a flat, "I'm not interested" at you early in the call.

Moreover, when you are successful in getting clients to say they have a need, they become interested right away. The identification of the need unleashes a desire on the part of prospects to learn more about it and to satisfy it. So instead of fighting the idea of participating in the call, customers are likely to assist in developing it further.

In consultative telemarketing, the emphasis shifts from *selling* momentum to *buying* momentum. In the last chapter you saw how that happened when the customer said to the rep: "Tell me about the bonus!"

So once needs have been uncovered, it becomes less likely that show-stopping objections will arise later in the call. This outcome is unlike that of traditional telemarketing, in which the closer you get to the close the more you can expect to hear objections. It's more likely because traditional sellers insist on doing most of the talking. In a sense, they are on "borrowed time," instead of being invited by the buyer to calmly continue the dialogue.

You'll find, in a consultative sale, that the customer may have questions or even concerns, but they are aired in a supportive way, if you have moved beyond the needs step.

If you haven't been able to establish a need, then the call should end, because you aren't going to have a solid reason to sell your product or service. So an objection that comes early, for the right reason, is actually a blessing because it is going to save everyone's time.

For instance, when I was doing some cold-calling to sell consulting services, I tried to elicit a need by asking a VP of a company if he wanted to increase his sales. "Actually," he replied, "sales are very strong. Our problem is that we can't keep up with demand."

Having heard this, I said, "That's a good problem to have," and I dialed the number of the next prospect on my list. You see, the VP wasn't "in pain," so I would be foolish to offer him medicine. A good doctor should find people who actually feel they need help. Those are the folks with whom phone conversations should be elongated.

DON'T MAKE "REJECTION" A PROBLEM

After you passed by a series of doors, and each one opened and someone threw a pie in your face, what would you do as you passed by the next door? You'd duck!

This is a natural way to react to negative reinforcement, and when telemarketers receive objections and customer resistance, that's what they're experiencing. Psychologically it feels punishing, and it's quite normal to try to avoid those punishments in the future. You may resist making sales presentations or asking people for their business because you're concerned that they'll reject you, and then you'll feel lousy about your abilities and yourself.

IMPROVE YOUR CLOSE

There are at least a few ways to take the sting out of rejection.

Try not to take it personally, as if prospects are rejecting you. They may be rejecting your message, but that's a different matter, because if your message is flawed, it can be revised or corrected.

If you're using an outline, call path, or script, you can note the places in the talk when things are bogging down and prospects are pummeling you. It might be a simple matter of revising your phraseology that will make a huge difference in reducing rejection and increasing sales.

For example, you can dramatically reduce your "No's," while increasing your sales with some refinements in closing phraseology. Experienced salespeople know that a reliable closing line can make the difference between getting an average and an exceptional number of sales.

Every now and then, a clear choice exists between using one of two forms of the same closing line. This can be seen in appointment-setting and in closing sales.

Say something one way, and you'll get 20 out of 100 prospects to say yes. Change the words slightly, and you'll close 30 or even 40 sales.

This choice exists when you have just finished describing your product or service and you're transitioning into the close. Most salespeople say, at that point, "What I'd like to do is ..." and follow with "see you on the 15th of November," or "send you one of our widgets on a 10-day trial." What sellers don't appreciate is the fact that they've allowed a weasel-phrase to creep into the presentation that is going to come between sellers and getting the appointment they want.

By saying what *you'd* like to do, you're stating a personal preference. Unless someone owes you a turn to get what you want, customers consider your needs irrelevant. Prospects generally owe salespeople nothing, so they couldn't care less about sellers' preferences.

Further, by inserting these words at this point, sellers invite the listener to make a yes-or-no decision prematurely. Instantly, on hearing that sellers want something, most prospects recoil into a defensive posture. Before hearing the caller out, they start rehearsing their knee-jerk "No" response.

If a caller's language worked backward, as it does for Yoda, the *Star Wars* character, using the like-to phrase might not be all bad. "See you on the 15th of November, is what I'd like to do ..." might arouse less rejection because prospects would be told, up front, what sellers were aiming at before hearing the like-to words.

But telemarketers are stuck with language the way it is, so how do they avoid this conversational booby-trap? Try saying, "What we're doing," or "What we'll do," in your phrase, instead.

In the appointment situation, sellers should say:

> What we'll do is stop by to say hello and get acquainted with your specific situation. The calendar indicates a good time to do that will be on the 15th of November, at 10; or will the 16th work out better for you?

This makes our visit sound like standard operating procedure and not something out of the ordinary, requiring a lot of evaluation to approve.

You'll find your sales shoot up when you employ the right phrases in closes, and rejection becomes much less of a concern.

FOCUS ON THE POSITIVE

Another way to diminish the impact of rejection is to systematically desensitize yourself to it. In other words, you can make it unimportant to you. It will continue to occur, but you'll have a thicker hide, so it'll hurt less.

Just as a public speaker who has stage fright should force himself to speak before lots of audiences, you can do the equivalent before sales prospects. Compel yourself to sell during every phone call. Instead of concerning yourself with your batting average — that you're closing 1-in-10 prospects — just count the total number of sales you're earning every day or week.

You'll see that the number soars because along with more rejections, you'll also inevitably get more sales. Seeing the increased sales, you'll minimize the emotional significance of rejections.

EMPLOY A NEW TELEMARKETING STANCE

The third thing you can do to master rejection is to adopt more of a consultative mode. You'll find that the number of rejections may diminish, but more important, their tone and tenor won't be nearly as aggressive or hostile as they are when we use traditional telemarketing.

LEARNING FROM THE OBJECTIONS YOU HEAR

I received a call the other day from a reader of my book, *You Can Sell Anything by Telephone!* He sells and installs home water-purification devices that affix to the plumbing and operate on a filtration basis And he has a problem.

Many of the prospects he talks to say that they purchase bottled water, and he doesn't know how to overcome this "objection."

His real problem is in treating the "bottled water" issue as merely an objection to his presentation or to his product. It's much more than that, and it requires an imaginative response that goes beyond a glib "answer."

In some respects, this seller's water filtration system competes with bottled water. After all, both promise to deliver cleaner, better-tasting H_2O. But this isn't the real problem.

He is asking his prospects to *change their buying habits*, and this is usually difficult to do.

If you take an early evening walk, during which you purchase a newspaper, it is going to be very hard for that paper or one of its competitors to sell you morning home delivery.

Your newspaper purchases are part of a larger lifestyle habit pattern. Buying the paper your way may be an excuse to get out after dinner, to exercise, and perhaps, to enjoy a little solitude.

The fact that the newspaper service will save you money and give you the utter convenience of home delivery is irrelevant. These aren't benefits to you, and they certainly don't address your apparent objection that you buy the paper at the newsstand. You might like talking sports or soaps with the newsstand proprietor, as well.

We all know that habits "die hard," and this is no less valid because we're speaking of buying habits. If you're going to try to change buying habits, you need more than a quick-fix, objection-focused approach.

The water salesman should build his entire presentation on the new concept for obtaining pure water. Communication theory suggests that a seller of filtered water should adopt a "two-sided" message strategy. This involves building the presentation to establish the many benefits of his innovative delivery system. It also requires using a reasonable sounding "attack" on bottled water.

It's the "build up and shoot down" method of selling. This is the best persuasive strategy for rapidly introducing an innovation that requires dislodging an entrenched competitor.

Don't wait for customers to offer you a classical objection if you know that they're in the habit of buying differently. Build all the information you need to deliver into your basic presentation, and you'll actually prevent objections from occurring.

AT ALL TIMES, APPEAR SELF-CONFIDENT
BY USING CONFIDENT LANGUAGE

I mentioned that the phrase, "What I'd like to do," will result in fewer appointments and more objections. There are several other *weasel words* that will injure your presentation while inviting rejection.

People, as a general rule, like to buy from others who seem to have self-confidence, as well as confidence about their products and services. Unfortunately, much of our everyday "street language" contains "iffy" weasel words and weasel phrases that project tentativeness and a substantial lack of confidence.

Here are some words to avoid using: *possibly, perhaps, maybe, potentially, could be, might be …*

And I'm sure there are others that you can think of. Here are some strong alternatives: *definitely, absolutely, undoubtedly, certainly, conclusively …*

People who lack confidence seem to constantly hedge in their language choices. On a basic, nearly animalistic level, prospects sniff fear in such weak language, and they strike out at its users through objections.

When you reduce — or better yet, eliminate — weasel words and phrases, you'll find that you *prevent objections*.

This chapter has prepared you to handle some of the toughest objections, both in terms of generating solid responses and in dealing with their psychological challenges.

In the next chapter, I'll help you to learn various ways to recruit, train, coach, counsel, and retain quality telemarketers.

You'll learn specific methods for attracting the best people through traditional advertising as well as through "creative" means.

You'll discover what I believe to be the best training methods for transforming nontelemarketers into effective telemarketers.

You'll see how training as well as coaching and counseling are continuous processes.

And you'll learn how some companies have cured the telemarketer-turnover problem. In our final chapter, I'll help you to address some of telemarketing's most perplexing questions and challenges.

CHAPTER SEVEN

RECRUITING, MOTIVATING, AND MANAGING TELEMARKETERS

To make an important point about hiring, allow me to re-tell a story I told earlier — but for a different reason.

When I had reached the wise old age of 18, I got my first office job as a telephone collector for a finance company. Little did I know that the basic skills I learned there would lead me to a career in phone work.

There was an unforgettable lady who worked on the telephone for the firm. I'm not a good guesser of ages, but I'd peg her as having been in her 70s. Her job was skip-tracing, which is a cross between being a detective and a bounty hunter. She'd call across the country trying to track down people who had left town and left a bunch of bills behind.

She was unique for several reasons. First, she wore fluffy, white, bunny-rabbit slippers. (I kid you not.) They matched her shock of white hair, which seemed electrified. Rail thin, she was almost a ghostly presence as she shuffled to and from the water cooler. She was very sweet to me, always making a point to give me a grandmotherly smile when she'd pass my desk.

What was completely incongruous about this lady, whom we called "Skip Tracy," was the fact that she was a telephonic powerhouse. Her phone manner was completely focused, and like the Canadian Mounties, more often than not, she "got her man."

As different as she was from me in age, gender, appearance, and manner, I could still relate to her. Just as she seemed to have two personalities — a face-to-face one, and a telephone version — I did, too!

Frankly, I was a little shy around businesspeople whom I had met in person. But on the phone, I could assert myself and get them to pay their past-due bills. The phone was a liberating medium for me because I could express aspects of myself that wouldn't emerge in the physical presence of others. I think this is why I was intrigued by it as a business tool as well as a medium for self-realization.

Of course, I'm recalling these stories for you as a way of introducing the topic of recruiting, developing, and managing telemarketers. Let me say, from the get-go, that there are few "silver bullets" in developing effective phone people, and some of the most unusual individuals can thrive in phone work, whereas the "sure-bets" that many of us have recruited have utterly failed.

For instance, if I told you to hire outgoing people who seem to have the gift of gab, I could be steering you in the wrong direction. As I parade before my memory all the truly great phone people I've known, strikingly few have been extroverts — or even aggressive, for that matter.

One was a soft-spoken jazz guitarist whom I recruited at Time/Life. His extraordinary gifts were his listening ability and his habit of shaping his voice to blend with those of his prospects. He memorized his script, enabling him to close his eyes and concentrate completely on the acoustical dimensions of telemarketing. An earthquake could rumble through the phone center, and he wouldn't budge until he had completed his conversation.

Another rep I cultivated had an exceedingly high IQ, so his tendency was to do anything but concentrate. Yet the repetitive nature of phone work gave him structure and routine, and I think it glued him together. His voice wasn't pleasant at all, but his sales figures rivaled those of the guitarist.

Two different people, with different strengths and weaknesses, both succeeded in telemarketing. I mention them because I'd like to help you to avoid falling into a classical recruiting trap: believing that there is a single "telemarketing personality," and if you simply find enough people who possess it, you'll be on easy street.

It just isn't so. No one can predict from a résumé, an interview, or even a social interaction, who will succeed and who will fail in telemarketing. As Peter Drucker has pointed out when speaking of employee recruiting generally, "No one is really great at it. We all make mistakes."

Of course, given the infamous levels of turnover found in telemarketing, many people would seem to be making more than their fair share of mistakes. As I noted in the first chapter of this book, it isn't unusual for companies to suffer through 400 percent to 1,200 percent annual turnover among telemarketers. I don't have to tell you that this figure is way beyond the norm for field sales and even for retail sales work.

So am I saying that it doesn't matter who you hire? Not at all. I'm going to show you how to recruit a steady stream of people, but even more important, I'll share with you some insights for helping them to succeed quickly and therefore to want to find a home in telemarketing.

THE TELEMARKETING TURNOVER PROBLEM

But before I get into these particulars, I want to share with you some of my ideas with respect to why telemarketing seems to have a tough time attracting and retaining good people.

Why would a reportedly well-managed Fortune 1000 organization tolerate 400 percent employee turnover, especially if it meant having to hire, train, coach, counsel, compensate, and fire 1,200 people every year?

There is a major metropolitan newspaper that does just that. And it's not alone. Countless firms, including telemarketing service bureaus, permit horrendous turnover in their telemarketing departments at staggering costs.

Estimates vary with respect to how much companies lose by quickly turning over employees. United Parcel Service pegs it at $5,000 per person. A telemarketing recruiting firm says turnover expenses run approximately 25 percent of the annual salary and benefits of an employee.

Using the $5,000 figure, the newspaper is wasting about $6 million per year by having to fill and refill 300 positions. It could be handing each of the 300 people $20,000 bonuses every year simply for staying aboard!

Why does this waste persist, and what can managers do to reduce it? To address telemarketing turnover adequately, leaders need to reengineer their model for staffing the telemarketing function.

Many telemarketing managers seem to suffer from a paradigm-lock that makes them think that rampant turnover is a necessary and even desirable aspect of telemarketing. They probably developed their telemarketing skills in an atmosphere of high turnover, yet they survived.

And in doing so, they have never stopped to question the fundamental belief that to build a telemarketing team you must have lots of losers for every winner who makes it. These same managers are probably proud of the fact that *they* could make it in what seems to be a survival-of-the-fittest atmosphere.

And so, like abusive parents who were the victims of abuse as children, telemarketing managers perpetuate the cycle of turnover without perceiving an alternative reality.

The first thing they need to realize is that incessant turnover *isn't normal*. It's unhealthy, and it needs to be cured. To improve, they have to step back and question the validity of their employee development routines.

What will a manager do if he believes that most of the people he's hiring are going to fail? Will he invest time and money in developing these individuals? Invariably not. And his disinvestment philosophy will seem rational. After all, why throw good money away on people who won't be around tomorrow?

This results in a vicious circle of failure. The surest way to make people fail is by leaving them alone to figure out how to do their jobs by themselves.

Most people can't perform the abstract thinking necessary to develop a winning work routine. They need mentoring and very accurate feedback to be shown how to do a job, and some take more time to develop than others. If managers tell them, "Sink or swim," most will drown.

What managers have failed to do is develop a proper methodology for helping the great majority of people to survive and thrive in telemarketing.

Some recruiters believe that they can succeed by hiring personality "types." This is foolish. There is no single personality-based predictor of telemarketing success. Actors, debaters, and other extroverts are no more likely to succeed than the shy type you'll find over in the accounting department.

Many firms try to increase the odds of success by sticking a written presentation in front of people while demanding that they bring it to life. Most of these pitches are one-sided talk-a-thons that customers reject.

They're like dumb bombs in warfare. Dumb bombs miss more targets than they hit. So, blanket-bombing is resorted to, just to assure minimal success. And blanket-bombing disturbs everyone, including telemarketers who are shot down by hostile prospects.

The answer to solving the turnover problem isn't in doing more of what we're used to doing. This would be like using a leaking bucket to carry water from a lake to and from a campsite. Simply scampering faster with the same buckets won't solve the fundamental problem of water loss.

To do that, you need new buckets. Or you need to move your campsite so it's closer to the lake. Or even better, you could consider building a pipeline that'll bring you water on demand without wasting a drop.

In other words, *only reengineering will reduce turnover in telemarketing.*

This requires us to change a number of processes and assumptions. In our consulting work we've put to work the New Telemarketing. It reduces turnover through the following principles:

- We have to pay telemarketers a living wage that's commensurate with field sales compensation. Mainstream people require mainstream pay. If you try to underpay, you'll only attract marginal and transitional people.

- Telemarketing should be full-time and not part-time work. Full-time work arouses a full-time commitment from managers and employees. People have enough time invested in the job to grow and develop. And they should receive full-time benefits, including healthcare coverage.

- Straight-commission compensation should be avoided, unless it is willingly negotiated by manager and employee. Most people feel they aren't really employed unless they receive some pay for their efforts even if they don't make sales.

- A conversational form of telemarketing should be emphasized. This is less stressful for buyers and sellers. It's also more likely to be needs-based, to sound professional, and to succeed.

- Telemarketers should have full account responsibility. If they've opened a new account through a cold-call, they should service the account and resell it in the future. This gives them an incentive to stay in the good graces of customers and to stick around for reorders.

- Significant resources should be invested in recruiting, training, coaching, and fully developing the capabilities of each person who is hired. In our consulting practice, we advise clients that they can expect to invest $2,500 – $3,500 per position to properly reengineer their telemarketing program.

Rampant turnover can be cured. But it has to be treated properly and thoroughly. One way to do this is through effective recruiting of phone personnel.

EFFECTIVE RECRUITING PRACTICES

There are three important things to do when recruiting for telemarketing work:

- Name the job properly.

- Effectively attract and screen job candidates.

- Value the job and sell its benefits to recruits.

In an earlier section, I mentioned that some organizations have decided to name their telemarketing units "teleselling." This is done, in some measure, to make the job attractive to job candidates.

You may find giving "telemarketing" another name will work well for you because many people avoid jobs with this term in their description. It may be necessary to use a little ingenuity in dubbing it something else.

NAMING THE POSITION

I did a recent survey of employment ads and uncovered 15 alternative job titles, which I'll discuss and briefly evaluate.

Telesales Representative

This isn't a bad name for the job, or for the work unit. Its advantage is that it puts candidates on alert that they are going to be asked to sell, which could come as a shock otherwise.

Inside Sales Representative

This is a widely used designation when a company has both outside, or traveling salespeople, as well as in-house people. Nothing wrong with the title, and it also tells candidates that they'll be selling.

Marketing Assistant

This is the first of several circumlocutions that are used to disguise the underlying work. Note that "telephone" doesn't appear in this name, and a marketing assistant could be someone who performs a range of clerical or persuasive duties.

The downside to this title is the word *assistant*. It definitely conveys a sense that the occupant of this job is junior in his or her status, which may not earn them the respect of their co-workers, clients, or friends and relatives.

Marketing Representative

This is similar, of course, to the last one, but it has a different set of meanings. First, a representative is usually someone who isn't hidden away from the world of customers. In fact, it is the person's job to connect the company to customers in some way. Thus, a job candidate could infer that the employee will have some communication duties, unlike the marketing assistant.

Telephone Consultant

I know, this one sounds confusing, doesn't it? It could be a person who sells phone equipment, or a person who offers consulting by telephone. What I like about it is the fact that *consultant* implies a degree of seniority and independent judgment, and so this dimension of the title could seem attractive to job candidates.

Telephone Sales Consultant

Well, the title suddenly became more specific, didn't it? If we simply dropped the word *telephone*, we'd be left with sales consultant, which is probably a higher status and less stigmatized title altogether.

Telephone Appointment Setter

Remember, my friend, I didn't devise these titles. They came from actual job ads! Of course, the person who responds to an ad for a telephone appointment setter knows exactly what the job entails, and I suppose that's a strength.

On the other hand, this sounds like a dead-end job to me. Is that *all* the person will be doing for the rest of his or her life? I think this title would deter some people from inquiring about the position.

Circulation Sales Representative

This is an industry-specific title that pertains to people who sell subscriptions to newspapers and magazines. It's not going to have much relevance elsewhere, but it does a good job of describing the job, while keeping the *telephone* word out of it.

Are there people who will apply, thinking that they're going to sell subscriptions door-to-door, or through some other means? Possibly. And this sort of confusion can result when the telephone word is not included. Moreover, you need to decide whether you'll waste your time setting up employment interviews with people who will grimace when they find that 100 percent of their time is going to be spent on the phone.

Customer Service Representatives

Before you think it is absurd to call a telemarketing job customer service, I should let you know that it's being done more often these days. This is partly the result of the fact that the once-sharp lines between service and selling are blurring.

But there is an even simpler explanation for why this title is used. It sounds helpful, and it is thought of in a positive way by nearly everybody. And, it'll certainly get the phone to ring with eager job candidates.

Again, the downside is the fact that there are service people who adamantly don't want to sell. And they could feel that they've been tricked into applying for what is mostly a true telemarketing position, which can ruffle some feathers.

Business Development Representatives

I like this one! It sounds dignified, and that is appealing. Obviously, there is going to be persuasion and selling involved in someone's activity when he or she operates under this moniker. It doesn't mention the phone, but it can be explained that "We develop our business by telephone" when people inquire about the position.

Here are some other titles that I saw less frequently. Some are hopelessly crass or vague, but you should see that they're out there, anyway:

- Telephone actors/actresses
- Closers
- Client reactivation specialist
- Tele-researcher
- Business development consultant

TIPS FOR ATTRACTING AND SCREENING CANDIDATES

Probably the most frequently used recruiting tool is classified advertising in the newspaper. There are several variables that you can control that will help you optimize this tool to get a better stream of qualified candidates to inquire about your positions.

Job Classification

Where in the classifieds should your ad appear? If you leave it up to the newspaper to decide, it will probably place your ad in the Telemarketing section. There are, as you might imagine, pluses and minuses to being located there.

You'll attract people who are attracted to telemarketing jobs, which means that many of them will be experienced. But if they are, you can bet that they'll have some interesting work habits that you'll either have to put up with or alter.

One rep who I hired insisted on jumping onto his desk when he was about to close a big sale! Apparently, this behavior was okay at his last place of employment. You'll find that experienced reps may join your team with certain verbal habits that are hard to break. And many of them may not want to stick to your well-worked-out presentation.

If it sounds like I'm saying it can be better to take novices and to mold them to your way of doing business, you're getting my point. So, I'd reluctantly allow my want-ads to be placed in the Telemarketing section, if I were you.

Sometimes you can convince newspapers to give you your own classification. For example, if you're in the newsletter publishing business, as I am, you might get them to run ads under the heading of Publishing. This could attract people who want to enter this industry.

You'll also probably have better luck in attracting good people if you advertise under these headings: Sales, Marketing, and Customer Service/Customer Sales.

Size of Ad

Ad size is significant. A large ad will attract disproportionate numbers of inquires. Yes, you can pinch pennies on smaller space, but you'll find that the larger ads breed confidence in your company.

Moreover, when you place large ads, you don't have to have an ad continuously running. You want to avoid the appearance of having a revolving door, where you're forced to keep your ads perennially in front of the labor market.

Graphics

Graphics count, too. It is usually a good idea to place your company's logo, especially if it's well recognized, somewhere in the ad. Again, this type of symbol arouses confidence because it makes your firm seem solid. Speaking of graphics, however, I'd avoid gimmicky illustrations, especially those that look like they're clip-art from a bygone era.

Timing of the Ad's Placement

More job seekers look at the Sunday papers than weekly and Saturday editions, so it's a good idea to run them on Sundays. Although the cost is higher, you should get a good return on your investment.

Frequency of the Ad

I think there is an inverse correlation between how often your ad runs and how effective it is. As I said earlier, you can send too much of a needy or flaky image to job seekers if they always see your ad. It devalues the opportunity you're extending.

The Job Description

It's common to list the duties to be performed by job candidates, and it's here that they'll get a glimpse of what they'll be doing if they come aboard. You have some choices to make in the language you use.

You may say, "You'll contact our clients," or you could be more explicit. "You'll phone our clients," will definitely reveal that phone contact is at the basis of the job.

I'd make a point of describing the communication practices of the ideal candidate. "You'll have an excellent command of spoken English and be able to communicate easily with senior executives, who are our clients."

Recital of Compensation

If you're offering a strong compensation package, by all means refer to it. But you don't have to mention specific dollar figures if you don't want to.

In fact, if you pay average or below-average wages, I wouldn't recite specifics in the ad. You are better off saving that discussion for the interview, when you can sell the compensation plan to qualified candidates.

The Employer's Name

Many ads, especially of the smaller variety, don't mention the company name. I would mention it, because I think it enhances credibility, and that way, you won't seem as if you're trying to conceal it.

The Employer's Location

As with so many variables, this can be a positive or a negative. If your firm is located on a beautiful business campus, the beach, or a lake front, by all means, mention it! My building is within walking distance of the Glendale Galleria, one of the largest indoor shopping malls in California, so I mention this fact in my ads.

If you're in a run-down section of town, leave this fact out of the ad.

Competing Ads

Don't place your ad in the same section that your competitors use if you can avoid it. Why go head-to-head with them, while inviting constant comparisons?

TAP SOME CREATIVE RECRUITING SOURCES

Effective as the classifieds can be, I think you'll find there are other venues and channels that you can use with great results. Here are a few "creative" recruiting avenues:

Job fairs

Your existing employees' referrals

Partnering with other employers

Employment agencies

School job boards and career offices

Religious and fraternal organizations

The Internet

Bulletin boards at car washes, grocery stores, and coin laundries

Handing out printed flyers

State, county, and local employment agencies and rehabilitation departments

How Should You Ask Job Seekers to Contact You?

I like to invite prospective telemarketers to call into voice mail. That way, I can cue-up their calls, listen to their messages at my convenience, and unobtrusively evaluate their communication capabilities.

I use a special, employee-intake version of my TEAMEASURES (Telephone Effectiveness Assessment Measures) to evaluate the quality of candidates' voices as well as their abilities to sell themselves for the job. (For more information about TEAMEASURES, refer to my audio training program, *Monitoring, Measuring, and Managing Phone Work*™.)

I'd avoid trying to hire people via résumés, because they don't reveal anything about the ability of a candidate to communicate using his or her voice. I'd also avoid "cattle calls," where you simply ask people to show up at a location between certain business hours.

Have candidates call into voice mail, and then, after evaluating them, call them back for further information. If they seem angry or resentful about their last employment experience, or if they pretend to be a Super-Phone Pro, I'd eliminate them from further consideration.

How to "Sell" the Telemarketing Job to Candidates

Some jobs don't need to be sold. When I consulted for an international airline, all my client had to do was run ads under "Airline" in the classifieds, and the human resources department was deluged with applicants. Frankly, most of the respondents didn't *care* what they'd be doing, as long as their pay plans included free-flight benefits for them and for their immediate families.

But I assume that you don't work for an airline or, for that matter, for a super-glamorous company. In the real world of employment, how can you make a telemarketing job sound wonderful to applicants who might have a prejudice against it?

Having "grown up" in telemarketing myself, I can say that there are many pluses to this job that you can stress:

- *It's a great job to have when you're going to school.* I put myself through many years of college and graduate school while holding down a telemarketing job. What I liked about it was the fact that it was steady work, and it didn't involve all that much change. Studying lots of new topics in school introduced enough dynamism for me.

- *It frequently offers flexible hours,* which are great for working parents, retired people, and for anyone with a major outside interest.

- *It is definitely a growing activity as well as industry,* so there are more career positions in management that are opening up all the time. And my contacts with executive search firms say there is a rapid upward movement of wages on the managerial level.

- For phone reps, *it often provides above-average compensation,* providing you are paid commissions or bonuses based on performance.

- *It is a great training ground for all kinds of careers.* I know people who attribute their success as a stockbroker or radio personality to their phone background.

TRAINING NEW TELEMARKETERS

Our language is filled with misleading dichotomies, such as the one that says, "Those who can, do; those who can't, teach."

This is a fictional statement because knowing and doing are interconnected. Perhaps the only way one can come to really know something, and therefore to later be able to teach it to another, is by doing.

We see this all the time in phone work, especially in telemarketing. The people who learn best are the ones who are put on the phones with "live" calls the fastest. They get a lot of battlefield experience, and they learn how to succeed under actual selling conditions.

If you want to discourage or greatly inhibit a telemarketer's development, prevent him or her from getting on the phones quickly. Keep the novice in lengthy lectures about products and company procedures. Give the new employee lots of rules to remember. And then, finally, weeks or months later, ask the telemarketer to put it all to work in real calls.

As a consultant, I battle this slothy approach all the time. At one mutual fund company, I had to convince an entire training bureaucracy that they were investing far too much time teaching details about products and industry before imbuing people with phone skills. What I could see, that they couldn't, was the fact that the longer you wait, the less effective the telemarketer will be when he or she finally hits the phones.

For one thing, a novice could easily develop an acute case of *communication anxiety*, also known as *phone fright*. I've observed that the longer it takes to get to the phones, the more concerned people grow about whether we'll be effective. This worry can lead to procrastination, to department-jumping in the firm (lateral transfers), and to outright employee turnover.

In the mutual fund company, before we reengineered the process, it took six months of training to get people on the phones. I cut that to six weeks, and several things happened. Turnover was slashed, and employee satisfaction soared. People learned to succeed by succeeding, and not by talking about success and through overpreparation.

Professional telemarketing firms understand this fact and put it to use. Many service bureaus recruit a person in the morning, train him or her in a two-to-four hour session, and have a telemarketer on the phones in the afternoon.

Although it's true that this novice could be woefully ignorant about the finer details regarding products and company history, he or she has rehearsed the script, and surprisingly, is probably capable of handling about 95 percent of all the conversational contingencies that will occur. He or she can fill in the remaining gaps in knowledge within a short time.

By "front-loading" telemarketing training, and "back-loading" product and company training, telemarketing firms are able to determine one crucial thing right away: whether the recruit has telephonic aptitude or is simply not cut out for phone work.

This saves time, money, and a lot of heartache for all involved. And it puts to work the truism that is so appropriate to phone work: *sellers learn by doing.*

COMPENSATION

Compensation is anything but a simple subject.

Obviously, people need to pay their bills, so whatever their rewards are, they need to help workers to satisfy this requirement. Therefore, people need a minimum of pay.

But compensation also has motivating and demotivating dimensions. For example, let's say that you're a part of a customer service team that has been asked to perform telemarketing. And you are the biggest producer, outselling everyone else by a wide margin.

But you're not paid anything extra for your exertions or for your sales results. How long are you going to bust your britches without recognition, in the form of some merit pay, commissions, or bonuses?

Not long, if you respond to the laws of human nature. As the great behavioral psychologists Pavlov and Skinner have said, behavior that goes unreinforced is "extinguished." In other words, your extra sales effort won't persist unless you're rewarded.

That only makes sense, doesn't it? Let's see the same scenario from someone else's point of view. Ernie, who camps out at the work station next to yours, doesn't even bother to up-sell or to suggestively sell, which you do all the time.

He sees you putting out a tremendous amount of voltage in order to make sales, while he just cruises. He thinks you're dumb for pushing yourself, because he knows that you're not earning an extra penny for it.

You can't help but hear him snicker every time you close a sale, while he asks you, with a whining, satirical voice: "Did you get *another* one?" His tone of voice drips with sarcasm, while sending the distinct message: "How can you be so stupid, you apple-polisher!"

Believe me, in that sort of negative environment, you aren't going to sustain your high sales output. Why bother? You'll slow down, or you'll find a job that does pay you for your performance.

What I'm saying is that companies that don't pay extra value while asking for extra output are foolish and are trying to contravene human nature. So a certain amount of pay-for-performance should be included in *all* telemarketing programs, whether they're performed by clerks, customer service reps, or people who are called "telemarketers."

Generally, I favor a base salary plus an increasing commission structure that is keyed to performance. This gives reps a certain amount of security, but it also rewards performance with appropriate amounts of pay.

In the next chapter, I'll discuss the pluses and minuses of "straight-commission" pay plans as I troubleshoot a question about the subject that is frequently asked in my seminars.

Planning an effective compensation program takes a good amount of thinking and flexibility, and it is one of the areas in which I consult. After all, you can train people all you like, but if you demotivate them instead of motivate them, you're not going to accomplish what you have set out to do.

I should point out that money is just *one* means of motivating telemarketers. Managers constantly wonder, "What are some new ways to motivate my people to give their greatest effort?"

So they try various incentives, such as contests. Rewards vary from "dinner for two" at some lovely restaurant, to paid vacations at exotic venues. A good number of people respond to these lures and turn in exceptional performances.

But there is one tried-and-true incentive that people truly appreciate, and it doesn't cost the company a fortune: *time away from the job.*

This can be as modest as a half-day to a full day off, with pay. It's desirable because the winners can customize it to suit their priorities. Mom or Dad might think it's great because they can watch their child play in a Little League game and really make a day of it.

Moments such as these are truly precious to parents, who too often can find themselves leaving their families at dawn and returning home nearly as darkness falls. To have earned some time off during the conventional business day can also enable people to take care of business on behalf of an elderly parent or simply do a little volunteer work.

Clearly, the potential uses for time off are unlimited, and that's what makes this reward a "new" one each time it is won. Moreover, it doesn't induce recipients to spend a lot to get it.

Often, when employees win a paid vacation to a specific venue, for instance, they find they have to dig into their own pocket for "extras." These can add up so much that they cost the winners real money — money that they'd never allow themselves to spend otherwise.

By comparison, the person who wins time off can economize and putter around in the garden, and find a sense of renewal that way.

There are some interesting consequences to providing time off based on merit. Those who win are less likely to use up their sick leave because of stress. After all, they give themselves a pressure release valve every time they earn time away.

So, why say you're sick, which bears a certain stigma, when you can use your "winnings" and be praised for it?

Some managers who consider time off as a reward express concern that they'll be losing the productivity of their best people. They ask, can't we just give them some money or prizes and still keep them on the job?

It's not the same, by any means. After all, these top performers earned their time away because of extraordinary productivity, didn't they? When they return, they'll have simply an added reason to work hard and to produce exceptional results.

They'll have recognition, refreshment, and an appreciation that their employer really knows how to reward them with what matters: a little money, and the time to do with it what they please.

MANAGING PHONE REPS AND PHONE WORK

Bud, one of your most experienced reps, seems unusually quiet. This has been going on for several weeks, yet it hasn't affected his production. You're concerned that he's having an impact on his work group, because new people seem to crawl into their own defensive shells and stay there. Their production is below normal. What's going on here, and what are you prepared to do about it?

This is a part of a case study that I discuss in my audio seminar, entitled *Monitoring, Measuring, and Managing Phone Work*. It presents the telephone sales center manager with a real problem. How can you manage this situation?

Usually, what I hear is that Bud "has a bad attitude." This may be true, but his attitude isn't impacting his own performance. So what can you do about it?

Almost everyone agrees we should sit down with Bud and talk it through. When we role play this meeting, nothing seems to get resolved. Bud says he's fine, and that you're imagining things. Anyway, are you really trying to link his attitude to the inadequate performance of your new recruits? That doesn't seem fair to Bud, and how defensible is this as a position for you to take?

This case, taken after a real situation that I faced as a young telemarketing manager, repeats itself every day in countless companies. Unfortunately, most managers make a classical error: they leap forward in an attempt to change Bud's attitude and to manage his personality.

Attitudes have three components according to researchers: (1) *cognitive*, or what we know about something; (2) *affective*, or how we feel about something; and (3) *conative*, or how we behave toward a situation. Managers err by trying to govern numbers 1 and 2.

Generally, this is frustrating and fruitless. Our only hope is to manage 3: behavior. We can establish a phone center code of conduct that will contribute to a generally positive atmosphere. For instance, someone like Bud could be torpedoing people's spirits by badmouthing customers.

It's common for people like Bud to say, after a call, "What an idiot that guy was!" Said in a loud enough voice, it'll definitely rock the boat.

Managers can formulate a rule that says, "We shall not badmouth customers in the phone center." If you prefer a positive cast to the rule, try: "We shall always speak well of customers."

This is an enforceable rule because it is expressed in behavioral terms. Managers can observe it, note when it has been violated, and confirm that they heard a violation by asking others if they heard it, too.

When people manage by an explicit code, they are no longer operating through suspicion and inference. By focusing on the behavioral component of attitudes, managers can control what they're really after: productive actions.

Managers intrude into an area that is off-limits when they try to play amateur psychologist with their people. My advice: Don't try to change how people think — simply concentrate on how they behave, and you won't drift too far afield. (For a sample code of conduct, see my audio seminar, *Monitoring, Measuring, and Managing Phone Work*.)

In the final chapter, I'm going to troubleshoot the 75 most-asked questions about telemarketing that I receive in my consulting work and in my live seminars. They run the gamut from how to read a script without sounding "canned," to the legality of the monitoring and taping of phone conversations.

I'm sure you'll find it informative!

CHAPTER EIGHT

ANSWERS TO TELEMARKETING'S
75 TOUGHEST QUESTIONS

It is my pleasure to share with you answers to some of the most frequently asked questions that I've encountered in my telemarketing consulting career and in my seminars.

I hope you'll find this information helpful and motivating! If you have any burning questions that aren't answered here, you can always contact me at the addresses or phone number that I've included in the Afterword, that appears at the end of this book.

1. How Can I Become a More Persuasive Telemarketer?

Build your persuasive abilities by becoming a devil's advocate. For fun, try to argue both sides of any idea or proposal. This will teach you to think like customers think while refining your ability to support nearly any idea.

2. How Can I Get Information from Customers Without Sounding Harsh or Like I'm Snooping?

If you want to get information from prospects, give information first. I call this "Telephone Communication Rule 1." People open up to others who self-disclose first. By the way, speedy disclosures accelerate the development of mutual trust and bonding.

It's a fact of life that people conceal information from someone they distrust. This is especially so on the telephone, because it is still, for the most part, a blind medium, and we are largely a visual culture. People distrust strangers whom they cannot see.

When you make cold calls and you have to get someone on the line whose name you don't yet know, you can easily arouse suspicions and evoke needless rejection if you do it the conventional way:

"May I have the name of the person who handles the purchasing of your office supplies?"

If you open your call this way, you're inviting a ton of negativity. You're announcing, right off the bat, "Look, I don't know you people from Adam, but I still want something from you."

"Just another grabby salesman in our midst," thinks the receptionist. "I'll jettison him to oblivion."

The problem with this opener is the fact that it violates one of the clearest communication rules of all time: If thou wishest information, giveth information first.

You need to, literally, open people up with your opener because they are typically clam-lipped to strangers. One of the best ways to loosen them up is to tell them that you have a legitimate purpose, perhaps that you want to provide a small service.

One winner that seldom fails is the "cleaning our mailing list" gambit: "Hello, this is Gary Goodman with Goodman Communications. We're trying to update our mailing list so we can reduce some clutter on your end. Who is the current VP of marketing, please?"

I've gone so far as to explain the call by saying it will help the caller to reduce the amount of junk mail the prospect gets, and people nearly always respond with, "Hallelujah!" They'll then give you the name of nearly everyone who works there. Of course, by providing you with the right name, you will be able to pinpoint your future mailings as well as phone calls.

Before telling prospects why you're calling, it's advisable to mention your name as well as the name of your firm. Nearly everyone wants to know with whom they're communicating, so tell them at the top of the call, and you'll spare yourself an interrogation.

It's amazing how forthcoming people are when you offer a brief and credible explanation for what you're trying to accomplish. It's well worth your effort, because you'll find you get what you want a lot more often.

3. How Can I Sound More Dynamic and Keep People's Attention During My Presentation?

Use power-packed phrases to sell. By making certain features and benefits sound vivid, you'll make them memorable and appealing. I devised a winning campaign for a specialty company by coining the phrase, "It's a gift within a gift." This phrase was very appealing and memorable to buyers because it contained a visual image.

4. IF I'M USING A TELEPHONE SCRIPT, HOW CAN I SOUND LIKE I'M NOT READING IT?

If you're using the phone to sell or to communicate with customers, "script" the routine parts of what you're going to say. But make sure to sound spontaneous by breathing in the *middle* of a phrase, and by reading in *phrases*, not individual words.

When people communicate informally, they constantly use jagged phrases here and run-on sentences there. Only when people read from a script do they clean it up, but it can be *too* tidy, and that's what can make us sound "canned." So, throw in an *um* every now and then, and you'll sound sincere and real.

5. I FEEL LIKE I'M WASTING VALUABLE SELLING TIME WHEN I HANDLE IRATE CUSTOMERS. IS THERE A WAY OF CUTTING THEM OFF?

I wouldn't advise that. Most complaining customers who gain sellers' attention are the loudest and the most demanding. They're the "squeaky wheels." Try to use the supportive language that I discussed earlier.

Also, pay attention to the minor complaints. There is a lot to be learned from customer complaints, and as you know from the camera-manufacturer example I provided, you can even turn complaints into new sales!

6. WHY DO A LOT OF OUR TELEPHONE PEOPLE WHO STICK TO THEIR SCRIPTS STILL FAIL?

Customers don't react to words alone. The text you use is important, and you should prepare it carefully. But you should also calibrate your tone and timing to support the text. You can use the best words in the world, but if your heart isn't in your tone, your words will fail to be persuasive.

7. HOW CAN CUSTOMERS TELL WHEN I'M READING FROM MY SCRIPT?

People can sense you're reading when your tone and text collide. When this happens, tone wins. If you sound bored, customers pick up on that and they stop listening to your words. You could be unwittingly sending a sarcastic message because of a tone and text conflict. Customers may not know how to respond to the conflicting messages they're hearing, so they simply attack your presentational style to escape from the call.

8. HOW CAN I GET MY COMPANY TO APPRECIATE THE IMPORTANCE OF TELEMARKETERS AND TO PAY US ACCORDINGLY?

Try to persuade management to "benchmark" your wages and benefits against those received by field salespeople. You'll earn a lot more money!

If you think you're being underpaid as a customer service rep or as a telemarketer, you may be in a world of company, but it can be changed.

Most phone workers in developed countries make approximately the same, generally low, wage. In cities, this amounts to $6.50 – $13.00 per hour (calculated in 1997 dollars), whether you dial and smile in Los Angeles or in London, England. Usually, the amount of pay is substantially less than what it takes for an individual to live independently on the economy, without support from parents, roommates, or spouses.

Phone pay, in customer service or telemarketing, is depressed because it is typically benchmarked against clerical pay. Yet this isn't always the case. Some phone jockeys make tons of dough, but they don't call themselves customer service reps or telemarketers. Instead, people know them as stockbrokers, bond salespeople, and talent agents. Gifted gabbers can literally phone their way to fortunes.

Let me remind you: David Geffen, the multibillionaire and show business mogul, got his start in the mailroom of a famous talent agency. As he would shuttle correspondence between executives, he'd observe how they handled themselves.

To his surprise, they all did the same thing. They "schmoozed" over the phone. He thought to himself, "I can do that!" And he did, with legendary success.

He forced himself to have 200 conversations per day by phone.

If one were to calculate the worth of an hour of his phone-time, it might be tens of thousands of dollars.

Some bond salespeople are rewarded nicely for sitting on the phone. Although they are paid on a commission-only basis, when they close a deal it can mean a big score. One fellow made a million-dollar commission in a single month by selling an investment to a bank.

An hour of his phone time proved to be worth about $6,000.

So, if you're an underpaid phone worker, there is hope. All you have to do is find an opportunity where you can put your teleskills to work.

Tip: You may want to avoid looking for a job that has the title "telemarketer" or "customer service rep." Instead, try looking under "talent agent" and "bond salesperson."

9. I'VE BEEN ASKED TO START A NEW TELEMARKETING PROGRAM. WHAT FORM OF COMPENSATION SHOULD I USE?

When you negotiate telemarketer and manager compensation, avoid offering or accepting a flat salary alone. Insist on providing some merit pay, commissions, or overrides in addition to fixed pay.

Show business negotiating is instructive. Actors like Gene Autry and studio moguls such as Michael Eisner have worked for modest salaries but have also insisted on receiving percentages of profits based on box office proceeds. Get your piece of the action, too, and you'll be happy you did!

10. How Can I Make the Best Use of My Phone Time and Multiply My Effectiveness When I Sell?

Use sales technologies to improve your performance. The fax machine, e-mail, and the Internet can be better media for transmitting literature than "snail" mail because they're faster in more ways than one. Your information arrives faster, but earlier transmission also promotes quicker buying decisions. This means you'll know where you stand with a prospect in a matter of hours or days, instead of weeks.

11. I Don't Like My Speaking Voice. Will This Hurt Me as a Telemarketer?

It's wise to practice your sales presentations with replay equipment, such as a tape recorder. Listening to yourself can give you valuable feedback about the unconscious vocal habits that you're introducing into sales conversations.

But don't judge your voice too harshly. People never sound as resonant when they hear a playback from a tape, as when they're just listening to themselves speak. You don't have to have a radio personality's voice to succeed.

Think of actor Eli Wallach, who has the grating voice you hear on Toyota TV commercials. I don't find his voice pleasant at all, and I'm sure he won't be offended by that, because his voice is *better* than pleasing — it's *successful*. It grabs your attention, which is just what Toyota wants to do when viewers watch the tube.

12. ISN'T THE TAPING OF PHONE CONVERSATIONS ILLEGAL?

If you plan to record an actual sales conversation, in person or over the phone, make sure to obtain everyone's consent. Otherwise, you could be breaking the law. Refer to my audio seminar, The New Telemarketing™, for extensive information about how to legally tape and monitor phone conversations. But in the meantime, here's an initial overview of this important subject.

Smart managers have known one thing since time began. If you're going to *expect* peak performance from people, you have to *inspect* their work. Find out what they're doing. Praise their strengths and help them to correct their weaknesses.

Unfortunately, you can't really improve phone work unless you find out what's going on in phone conversations. You need to listen to conversations — both sides of them. This necessitates monitoring or taping calls.

However, nonconsensual monitoring or taping of calls is illegal in at least 13 states, and if the threatened federal legislation passes, it will be illegal everywhere.

California's Penal Code Section 632 is typical of such restrictions. Called the Invasion of Privacy Statute, Section 632 makes it a crime to monitor or record the conversations of people without their consent. Penalties include a $2,500 fine and a year in county jail or state prison. This crime can be filed either as a misdemeanor or as a felony. Repeat offenders are faced with even stiffer penalties.

There are many misconceptions about the circumstances under which one may or may not intrude on calls. Here is a sampling:

- Some managers foster the belief that "if the monitoring or taping is done for training purposes only, it's okay." Not true. Section 632 is not a specific-intent crime, which means your frame of mind is irrelevant. By analogy, if you're caught doing 85 in a 45-mile-per-hour zone, your lack of intent to speed is of no concern to the cop who tickets you.

- Many people confuse "notice" with "consent." They think it's okay to intrude on calls if people know what's going on. Big mistake. Lots of banks and other large firms announce at the beginning of calls that callers might be monitored or be taped. This notification falls far short of obtaining someone's voluntary permission for the intrusion. Consent means notice *plus* voluntary approval.

- Some folks think that you can simply have an electronic "beep-tone" chime into the conversation every so many seconds and this will enable you to monitor or tape. Not true. Lots of people have no idea what the beep means, so you don't even achieve "notice," let alone consent.

- "It's no big deal to break the law because it's seldom enforced." Baloney. There are prosecutions under Section 632, and even if there weren't so far, would you like to be the first one?

- "The penalties, even if you're tried and convicted, are minimal." This is a huge misconception. How many calls do you monitor or tape in a single day? Firms that tape all their calls through a centralized switch could be guilty of committing hundreds of punishable offenses every day. How much is 100 times $2,500 and 100 times one year in prison? Get the picture? Every call can constitute an offense.

- "No one would want to prosecute us — we're pillars of the community." Your firm could be the corporate equivalent of Mother Teresa and still get into trouble. Look around. Lots of prosecutors, attorneys general, city attorneys, and district attorneys are politicians. They need popular issues with which to get elected and reelected. Huge voting blocks hate telemarketing, such as folks represented by the American Association of Retired Persons (AARP). They feel victimized by telemarketing and they would embrace as a hero a politician who could shut down phone centers. And older folks vote!

- "If one law says it's okay to tape or monitor, then it's okay." Any lawyer will tell you that on a given day it's very difficult to discover what *the* law is, because there are numerous laws and sources of law that govern our conduct. For instance, the Federal Communications Commission (FCC), which has some authority over phone conversations, is concerned only about one-party consent to monitor or tape calls. But the FCC can't and won't speak for your state, which can pass a law similar to California's Privacy Statute. The California Public Utilities Commission may say that it's okay to monitor or tape with a beep-tone, but Penal Code Section 632 does not agree.

- "If my firm isn't in California or in one of the jurisdictions that requires all-party consent to monitor or tape, I'm free to do what I want." Wrong again. If you call into California, or if Californians call you, and you perform the offending activity, you can be hauled into California's courts.

- "If monitoring or taping is so bad, why do firms like Radio Shack continue to sell 'telephone pick-ups' and devices for tapping into calls?" Gun shops sell guns, but you are punished for pulling the trigger.

- "I've delegated this issue to Mary Ann, my telemarketing manager, and it's up to her to figure out what we can or can't do." Don't let Mary Ann practice law without a license. There is no substitute for consulting with a lawyer if you want legal information or advice.

Unfortunately, 99.9 percent of practicing attorneys will tell you, after reading Section 632, to "stop monitoring and taping — period." They won't tell you how to monitor or tape within the parameters of the law and to do so in a way that won't offend customers or employees.

Yet as a good manager you may feel that listening to calls is the best way to lead your people into higher realms of achievement. This could put you into a bind. If you do what you feel is right as a manager, then you could be a criminal; and if you don't monitor or tape, you could be an irresponsible manager.

Happily, there are scripts for complying with the law that don't negatively impact your phone conversations. Telemarketers have crafted conversational ways to enable phone people to obtain consent from callers, prospects, and customers, both on inbound as well as outbound calls.

I discuss these techniques in detail in my New Telemarketing Audiocassette Seminar.

13. DO REPS SELL MORE WHEN THEY'RE SITTING IN PRIVATE OFFICES OR IN A COMMUNAL PHONE CENTER?

If you're using the phone to sell or to set appointments and can choose to make calls in a private office or in a communal "bullpen," choose the bullpen. The lively atmosphere of working with other salespeople will lessen your inhibitions with customers, and some friendly competition will serve everyone's purposes.

For many of us, work is an important social environment as well as a place to earn a paycheck. Making friends, comparing notes about life, and celebrating birthdays and employment anniversaries become rituals that give people a sense of meaning and belonging.

It may be for social reasons as well that phone workers seem to perform better in a bullpen environment than off by themselves on the sidelines, in separate offices. Salespeople sell more and customer service people perform faster and with higher morale when they're surrounded by like-performing peers.

Telecommuters also complain of loneliness when they work from home, far from the water cooler chit chat. They identify less with company goals than their on-site peers and feel more as if they work for themselves.

People who voluntarily leave organizations to go out on their own often have trouble adapting to the solitary home-office life. Some escape their new digs and drag laptops and cell-phones to coffee bars just to feel plugged into the rhythm of the outside world. Many never adapt; their ventures fail, and they return to the comfort of a group atmosphere.

Working alone can create a feeling of anomie, or normlessness. Without the formal and informal controls that come from working with others, people can feel unguided and out of synch. Left to create and to sustain their own work routines, people can waste time with minutiae, simply because they don't have peer or management pressure to perform otherwise.

Ironically, one of the lifelines that solitary workers might look to for comfort and support is another telephone-based source: the Internet. By joining dialogues on-line, remote workers can speak to each other, share stories, and pep each other up when necessary.

As more companies explore the advantages of having workers perform away from headquarters, they'll need to find surrogates for the interpersonal communications that people enjoy the most about working inside organizations.

14. Do the Best Sales Incentives Always Involve Cash Prizes?

If you have input into the rewards offered in sales contests, provide for paid time off as well as cash awards. It will help reps to recharge their batteries and encourage them to take well-deserved vacations.

15. What Should I Do When a Customer Praises Our Product or Service?

When a client says that he or she is happy with your product or service, ask the client to elaborate. When you hear a great endorsement, repeat what you've heard, and ask: "May I quote you on that?" This way, you can multiply the impact of someone's word-of-mouth advertising by inserting it into your future sales talks and your promotional literature.

16. DOES IT PAY TO USE PRODUCT GUARANTEES WHEN TELEMARKETING?

Yes, you'll increase sales volume with guarantees, but don't rely on them too much. People should be buying because of the underlying needs that your product serves, not simply because they can "undo" a sale if they aren't happy.

Often, guarantees will help you to close sales that you wouldn't get otherwise. In other cases, they may coax you into selling people who are "flaky" and who don't justify your sales effort.

Guarantees are becoming a way of life in sales and marketing. Everywhere you turn, there seems to be one. Recently, a seminar company offered a lifetime guarantee, if you can believe it. It said, "If you ever come to feel that this course wasn't wonderful, we'll give you your money back!"

Imagine, 90 years from now, waking from your all-day nap to discover that the French Cooking class you took nearly a century before let you down. Never could master that darned soufflé! Why not get a refund? Even McDonald's, the icon of value, has used guarantees to tout its burgers and new menu items.

How effective are guarantees as sales tools, and when should you use them? Guarantees can build sales very quickly, because they can persuade the tough prospects, as well as get customers to spend more than they anticipated.

When do you need one? I suggest using a guarantee when *you're the new kid* on the block. A guarantee might do you a lot of good if you're just starting out and having to fight entrenched competitors. How do you get people to try you out?

By taking the financial risk out of it, and this is what a guarantee accomplishes. Hampton Inns took the lead in this area a few years ago by offering a money-back guarantee for the first night's stay if the lodger found it unsatisfactory. This was a way to earn major attention for a new national chain while asserting a quality pledge that differentiated itself from its many competitors.

Also try using one when there's been *negative publicity* or bad word of mouth about your product. You might need a guarantee to reassure people who are interested in buying from you, but who are afraid.

The Jaguar automobile is an example. I've never met anyone who isn't impressed with the looks of a Jaguar. But, as *The Wall Street Journal* has reported, owners often have mechanical nightmares with it.

A few years ago, Jag responded by offering the public a 30-day free test drive. Other car companies, like Audi, have gone further by offering full-maintenance contracts along with their cars. These promotions don't last long. I sense that short-term expedients are used to restore a sense of confidence. After they've succeeded, guarantees are abandoned.

A third reason to use one is when your product or service is a true *innovation*. One of my clients is the fellow who sold the Berlin Wall, one tiny piece at a time. Remember those little rocks glued onto plaques a few years ago in department stores? His idea. He sold a million of them in six months. They came with certificates of authenticity. Another name for guarantees.

Use a guarantee when your product or service *changes customers' buying habits.* The same client who sold the Berlin Wall came to me with a new product he wanted to market that purifies water one drop at a time, through a handheld, pen-like dispenser.

He asked me my opinion and I told him it would be marketable only with an unconditional guarantee, because folks weren't used to buying pure water that way. They're used to bottles and filters.

Federal Express, with its 10:30 A.M. overnight delivery guarantee, is another example of an innovator having to use a guarantee when it invented overnight delivery service. Could you sell Christmas trees or puppies or kitties by phone or through mail order? Probably not without a guarantee, because you're changing important buying rituals and sentimental traditions.

You'll also need a guarantee when you're selling *sensory products* that usually appeal to a prospect's taste, touch, or vision. Fine art and vintage wines come to mind. A guarantee might substitute for someone proving to herself with her own senses the value of your offer. If you want to substitute telemarketers for field salespeople, you might have to arm your phone people with guarantees as well.

Winning back lost customers can necessitate the use of a guarantee. After all, why should clients risk disappointment or failure with you, again? Bankrupt airlines attempting to return to normal service will dabble with satisfaction guarantees for this reason.

Another circumstance is when the *risk of loss* is high or defects are not subject to inspection. Big-ticket items call for guarantees. That's why most cars, houses, and computers are sold with warranties.

When your *margins are high*, consider using a guarantee. Your additional sales will more than compensate for your losses from returns.

You should offer a guarantee only when your company culture will tolerate product returns, refunds, and their operational demands. Some companies are too egotistical or too temperamental to accept product returns.

One of my clients owns photography studios across the country. The studios offer a guarantee, but they're utterly miffed if clients exercise it — and they show their contempt openly.

They hire people who believe they are part of the high-fashion industry, and their haughtiness is very thinly disguised. My suggestion to them is: either make it easy to use the guarantee or stop offering it altogether. Other firms, like Nordstrom, have built dynasties on unconditional — and often wildly generous — guarantees. And their patrons truly seem to appreciate them.

Use guarantees when there are *stop-losses available*. Use guarantees to sell personal services only when you can stop your losses before completing the entire service. If you're in a CPA firm, work up a client's numbers but don't fill out the tax return before getting client approval. If you're a barber, stop after cutting the left side of the head — just kidding. You can see why service guarantees have problems.

Again, guarantees will certainly earn you additional sales. They'll also have an interesting impact on how you do business. When you strongly assert a quality guarantee, you have to build your product or service so it lives up to buyer expectations. This imposes a quality frame of mind on your firm. Suddenly, you have an announced, challenging standard to live up to. But achieving a higher level of satisfaction will win customer loyalty and higher profits.

17. It's Difficult to Return All My Customers' Calls. It Takes Me a Few Days to Get Back with Them. Is That a Problem?

Remember that it's "the little things" that drive customers nuts and straight into the arms of your competitors. Try to return phone calls immediately, no matter where you are. It is still one of the benchmarks of great service, and prompt callbacks seldom fail to impress your toughest customers.

Call back even if you don't have time to have a lengthy chat. Simply stay in touch. Clients get a queasy feeling if you frequently seem to disappear from the face of the earth.

If you're really too busy to make your callbacks, it may be time for you to hire an assistant!

18. Some Salespeople Send Out Newsletters and Small Items to Their Clients. Do People Really Appreciate These Gimmicks?

Try to give every effort to making small but significant gestures that tell your clients that they are important. Keep them on your company's mailing lists. Remember birthdays and anniversaries if you can find out what they are. Send holiday cards, thank-you notes, and faxes. The list of little things that you can do is endless.

19. I've Been Told That the Best Thing to Do When a Prospect Says No Is Just to Call the Next Prospect. Do You Agree?

That's generally sound advice because it does no good to dwell on the naysayers. However, if you've been courting an important prospect and you lose out to a competitor, it makes sense to conduct post-mortems, or post-presentation interviews to see what you did right or wrong. By asking the nonbuyer to critique you and your firm, you'll make your wins *and* your losses pay off.

20. SOMETIMES I FALL INTO SALES SLUMPS, AND I DON'T KNOW WHY. WHAT DO YOU SUGGEST?

If you are having difficulty selling, ask yourself how *you* would like to purchase your own product. By phone? By fax? By mail? In person? Through a combination of the above? If you're not doing what you would like to have done, you're missing the mark. Calibrate your approach to suit the customer.

21. HOW CAN I TELL WHETHER MY COMPANY IS TELEPHONICALLY EFFECTIVE OR INEFFECTIVE?

Try calling "yourself" on the phone. How does the company receptionist treat you? That's the first impression that he or she is making on your behalf! Make sure it's an effective one.

22. I SELL A COMMODITY THAT IS INDISTINGUISHABLE FROM THOSE MY COMPETITORS SELL. HOW CAN I MAKE MY PRODUCT UNIQUE?

Try to stand out in buyers' minds by doing something very old or very new. For instance, when you write to them, you might occasionally try using personal, high-quality stationery. If your handwriting is legible or especially attractive, you can make a lasting impression by using it, instead of formal-looking (impersonal) type.

23. WHAT'S A SUREFIRE WAY TO GET NEW PROSPECTS TO TRY OUR PRODUCTS OR SERVICES?

Sometimes you can win new business by giving away "free samples." This works well in the food industry, as well as in certain service businesses and professions. It's worth experimenting with.

24. WHAT'S THE DIFFERENCE BETWEEN TELEMARKETING AND TELESELLING?

For the most part, the terms are interchangeable.

Some companies and individuals prefer the sound of the term *teleselling*, and they feel it reflects more closely the nature of the work that is done in that department.

Telemarketing can be a broad term and include selling, lead generation, appointment-setting, prospect qualification, list-updating, and other functions beyond traditional teleselling.

25. I'M AFRAID I'LL STARVE IF I ACCEPT A STRAIGHT-COMMISSION TELEMARKETING JOB. SHOULD I BE WORRIED ABOUT THIS?

Commission-only telemarketing jobs can be great, take it from me. When I was finishing my Ph.D., I held one down, part-time, in addition to my teaching duties. It helped me to live much better than your typical graduate student/college professor. But it's not a good fit for everybody.

Recently, I was phoned by a woman who was dissatisfied with her appointment-setting job at a nearby company. Asking if my firm had any positions available, I replied that we did.

She sounded poised enough to do well in business-to-business telesales. We discussed the job, and she seemed genuinely excited, and an interview was set for three days hence.

Within a few hours, she phoned back to cancel, saying "My husband doesn't want me doing a straight-commission job." This isn't unusual. Straight-commission jobs that pay only for results and not for effort are intimidating to the great majority of people.

But they could become the wave of the future, not only in sales, but in many other kinds of work. Teachers, for example, could be paid according to how successfully their students pass standard competency examinations. Here's how straight-commission plans operate to benefit both employer and the employed:

By paying only for results, businesses must define precisely what "results" are. There are still many jobs that are so vaguely characterized that workers and managers don't really know what below-average, average, good, better, and best performances are.

The same job candidate that I just mentioned said she was promised an hourly wage and a bonus by her current employer. She received the hourly, but the bonus never materialized. She is now paranoid that she'll be taken advantage of by other bosses.

The psychologist B. F. Skinner said, "Behavior is a function of its consequences." You get what you pay for — period. If you pay for someone's time, you'll get their time, and some effort. If you pay for results, you're more likely to get results. The key is to reward the right thing.

Parkinson's Law seems to apply to salespeople who are paid mainly for their investment of time. Parkinson says the time it takes to complete a task is proportionate to the time allowed for the task's completion. The salaried worker actually has an incentive to take *longer* to get sales.

Of course, that makes the salesperson's relationship with an employer an adversarial one. A rep can "win" through sloth, whereas the house loses. The boss wants to speed up the worker because then the cost of the sale declines. But the worker wants to slow down because the value of the sale then increases for him.

The key to a rational compensation scheme is to align the interests of the worker with the employer, and straight commissions can do just that.

The overall costs of managing a straight-commission plan are lower than an hourly or a salaried plan. Policing costs are higher with a time-based pay plan, because bosses need to be assured that their people are performing work. Overseers are needed to watch the production process, and the overseers often need overseers.

With straight commission, the reward, itself, is the control on worker behavior. If you know that your success is what determines your level of pay, you're going to eschew distractions and focus primarily on the task at hand.

Straight-commission plans shift the focus from a company-sponsored "training" emphasis to a worker-sponsored "learning" emphasis. If workers don't earn money while they're training, they have an incentive to learn fast and to put their knowledge to work even faster.

If they're paid to sit in classrooms and to zone-out while gazing at flip-charts and overhead projections, they'll do that. It's easier than selling.

Straight-commission jobs can be, and often are, more lucrative. If employers have a finite pool of money to pay for sales, members can direct its flow to achievers. In a pay-for-time arrangement, the pool of rewards is siphoned off to nonachievers, which diminishes the prize for the winners.

It's demotivating for achievers to observe that laggards earn the same as they do, or close to it. Inevitably, the racehorses slow down to match the pace of the plodders. In exasperation, they ask themselves, "What am I busting my saddle for?"

Managers don't have to terminate nonperforming commission salespeople. Generally, they terminate themselves, if the rewards aren't forthcoming after a reasonable amount of time and effort.

However, managers can afford to allow commission-only salespeople to develop more slowly, if that's what it takes. Because businesses have a lower financial investment, they can afford to be patient until their new recruits succeed.

I spoke to a telemarketer who works from her home on a straight-commission basis. She makes calls when her two-year old naps. It has taken her three months to earn her first commissions, which is a long time to go without pay for one's efforts. But her employer could afford to wait, because she is responsible for much of her overhead.

On a philosophical level, the straight-commission formula comports with the underlying realities of a capitalistic economy. Sooner or later, people are paid for what they produce.

Noncommission pay plans temporarily disguise this fact, making it possible for nonachievers to be rewarded for lengthy periods before their nonresults are audited and addressed.

It seldom comes as a shock when a commission salesperson is terminated. Usually, he or she is keenly aware of how it's been going, while the rep is honing work skills to make his or her contributions and rewards even greater.

You should try to find a sales job in which you make sales at a comfortable rate. That way, you'll see regular paychecks, whether they're based on salary, commissions, or a combination of both.

I've consulted for companies that sell tractors, combines, and other heavy farm machines. Each salesperson may sell only two or three per season. Because the machines cost so much, this production level is sufficient to pay commissions and to provide the business with a return on investment. But it takes patience to wait for the sales to close.

If you need more frequent positive reinforcement than this, don't sell agricultural equipment! Smaller-ticket sales may be better for you, whether you're salaried or commissioned.

26. WHY DO ACTORS AND PERFORMERS SEEM TO DO SO WELL IN TELEMARKETING?

They adopt a "show must go on" mentality about selling.

For instance, I was scheduled to be interviewed by NBC's hit show, "Dateline," one day. That morning I broke my foot when I went jogging. I hobbled home and showered and still did the show, although I was in great pain.

Doing the show was important to my marketing effort. It was like delivering a product after it has been sold. I simply forced myself to do it.

By becoming disciplined in this way, you'll develop great emotional strength and probably become a top telemarketer, whether you've had showbiz experience or not.

27. HOW CAN I STAY MOTIVATED?

Try saying a little prayer before you call your next prospect. You don't have to be a religious person for this to give you a sense of inner peace and positive expectations.

28. DO HAPPY-GO-LUCKY PERSONALITIES FARE BETTER IN TELEMARKETING?

Buyers *do* seem to favor cheerful people with their business. To keep your spirits high, develop a sense of humor. Smile when you greet people by phone or in person. Your good cheer will be beamed back to you, time and again.

29. HOW CAN I CURE THE CASE OF "BUTTERFLIES" THAT I GET BEFORE I TELEMARKET?

Channel your fear. Fear is energy that is self-directed. Turn the fear outward. Make your jitters your helper. Call on them to transform themselves into enthusiasm and positive results.

30. HOW CAN I MAINTAIN A POSITIVE MENTAL ATTITUDE ABOUT TELEMARKETING?

Monitor your self-talk. Does the little voice in your mind say things like, "I'm tired," and "This will be tough to sell"? If you hear negatives, just say "Cancel that!"

Dispute debilitating self-judgments. Substitute phrases such as: "I'm not tired. My energy is dipping, but it'll come back, multiplied!"

Here's another positive thing to tell yourself: "This prospect could be difficult, but I'm prepared to handle anything. For me, this call will go just right. I'll do very, very well."

31. HOW CAN I RAISE MY SALES AVERAGES? THEY ALWAYS SEEM TO STAY IN THE SAME ZONE OF ACHIEVEMENT.

Imagine earning a larger specific number of sales before each day or shift begins. Be precise in your goals!

When I sell my products, I tell myself: "I'm going to get five sales before dinnertime!" Then, as my day unfolds, I check my progress against this numerical target.

I find it helps to write down my numerical goal; this gives me a visual reminder to goad me on to better performance.

32. WHAT'S YOUR BEST NEGOTIATING TIP?

If a new customer tries to get you to deliver a dramatic discount on an initial sale by enticing you with promises of higher volume business in the future, be skeptical. This is frequently a negotiating ploy.

If you discount the first sale, you'll either have to deeply discount the rest, or there were no more sales planned by the buyer, who was misrepresenting his or her intentions to by "in volume" in the future. Few buyers will let sellers recoup their foregone profits on initial sales.

33. HOW CAN I KEEP UP WITH MY TELEMARKETING WHEN I'M ON THE ROAD?

If you need to travel long distances to see clients, by car or by air, don't skimp on the amenities. Stay in decent hotels that cater to business travelers. And whenever possible, join airline and hotel clubs to earn or be given free upgrades. Use a laptop with a modem, carry a cellular phone, and buy a fax package to keep in touch with the office and to stay on top of deals with clients when you're away.

34. WHAT'S ONE OF YOUR BEST TIME-MANAGEMENT TIPS?

You'll get more done, with a better disposition, when you handle the toughest tasks at the beginning of the day. If you don't, they'll burden you, and you won't perform other tasks with enthusiasm.

Don't put off calling an irate or difficult client. Get it done, A.S.A.P., and you'll lift a great burden from your shoulders.

35. SHOULD THERE BE A DRESS CODE IN MY PHONE CENTER?

Even if there is no formal dress code where you work, you may want to enforce your own personal dress code. Do you work better, and produce more, when you're wearing formal business attire? Many people are like this, yet they "dress down" if their companies allow casual outfitting.

You may look like a geek to other people if you wear your three piece suit and tie while others are wearing jeans, but that's their problem. Dress in a manner that makes you feel right, and you'll sell more.

Designers are telling us that we're becoming a less formal culture and our clothing preferences are reflecting this attitude.

They're saying that "dressing-down" is becoming a national trend. Necktie-optional workplaces for men are becoming more common in places far from California and Hawaii, pioneers of casual living.

Phone centers — especially those engaged in telemarketing — have been fashion renegades for decades. Kelly-Springfield Tire Company used to house its telemarketers in a separate building, where they could look individualistic and not upset the rank and file.

Many industries began without dress codes and have struggled to stay that way. Software firms often cut a lot of slack for developers and for those in tech support and customer service who don't see customers on a day-to-day basis.

I recall consulting to one software company while I was dressed in jeans, boots, and a sports shirt. My client was located at the beach, so it was an unwritten perk of the job for people to dress as they pleased. In a sense, they could embody the casual lifestyle around them.

Nonetheless, dress codes have their advocates. "People should be reminded they're at work," one customer service manager declared, when the subject came up in one of my recent seminars on "Monitoring, Measuring, and Managing Phone Work."

Supporters of this view maintain that formal business attire gets people into the mood to work and adds to their feeling of professionalism. They seem more serious about their work.

And if they're on the phone, some managers claim they even sound better. Crisp. Prepared. Disciplined, if you will.

Of course, there is an important economic dimension to requiring formal business attire. It costs workers a substantial amount of money. When wardrobe purchases and dry cleaning are calculated, traditional business attire can run into thousands of dollars per year.

Being free from conforming to a dress code is also a form of comfort-compensation for some workers. It gives them "psychic income" that may induce them to stick around longer than they would otherwise.

Others say they don't really feel they're employed unless there are clear reminders of this fact, as there are by having to don "uniforms."

Determining whether to adopt a restrictive dress code in a phone center is a tough decision. Changing an existing clothing policy can be even tougher.

A manager at a publishing firm, who was new to the company, burst on the casual scene and announced that henceforth suits and ties for men, and skirts for women, were required. Within a few weeks, 50 percent of the phone workers quit.

So, devising or enforcing a dress code should be much more than a "casual" decision.

36. HOW SHOULD I PREPARE FOR TELEMARKETING?

Remember to do several things. (1) Have an extensive calling list. You never want to run out of names and phone numbers to call. (2) Call everyone on the list. Don't prejudge people by their names. (3) Don't stop when you hear bad news or when you're stung by rejection. (4) Remember that selling is a numbers game. The more calling you do, the luckier you'll get.

37. LOTS OF PEOPLE ARE TELEMARKETERS WHO DON'T BEAR THAT TITLE. IS THIS RIGHT?

If you use the phone to persuade other people, you're doing telemarketing as far as I'm concerned. But you don't have to be referred to as a telemarketer, if another label would better serve your purposes.

Try to negotiate the most impressive-sounding occupational title from your company that you can. This isn't for the purpose of impressing friends and neighbors, though you might. It is to impress secretaries and receptionists. A firm that I consult for has anointed many of its six-figure earning salespeople, "senior vice president."

This title looks great on a business card, but it also sounds great when you call a mucky-muck: "Hello, I'm Gary Goodman, Senior Vice President with Bozometrics ... ."

38. I'm Afraid That I'm Going to Sound Really Stupid When I Start Telemarketing. What Can I Do to Avoid This?

First of all, be kind to yourself and try to control your perfectionistic tendencies. You don't have to be flawless or even great to succeed on the phone. Try hard, stick to the basics, and don't sideline yourself with worries, and you'll be fine.

As a matter of fact, sometimes openly acknowledging your beginner status can be a plus. When you first start out in telemarketing and even later on, for that matter, make a strength out of your ignorance. How can you do that?

By not pretending to know it all and by leveraging a prospect's goodwill and natural desire to be of assistance. I've had tremendous success cold-calling with these opening words: "Hello, Mr. Smith, I'm Gary Goodman with Melville Associates, and I'm calling because I was hoping you might be able to help me out … ."

Most prospects will say, "Okay," or "I'll try." In other words, they'll cooperate, and you will have taken some pressure off of yourself to sound 100 percent polished.

Recall those golden words of a very successful marketing V.P. for a training company. He described the best attitude to have when interacting with customers: "'Nice and humble does it every time!'"

39. Are Scripts Inevitable in Telemarketing?

In a word — yes. Sooner or later, you'll probably end up using a script for selling. Why do I say this? Even when you don't think you're using a patterned talk, there are repeated fragments that crop up from call to call because your unconscious believes these phrases have worked for you before.

You'd be making a mistake to think of all scripts as phony or ineffective. They are as natural as language. I suggest you think through certain phrases and selling sequences in advance, then test their effectiveness.

I know a successful salesman who was taught to prepare a few golf stories that he could share with prospects in order to break the ice. He found they did the job, and he earned more sales as a result. Of course, those stories were carefully scripted.

40. WHAT PHRASES WOULD YOU AVOID WHEN TELEMARKETING?

There are several phrases to avoid. One of them is, "What I'd like to do ... ." It emphasizes your wishes and, in doing so, seems to elevate your priorities above those of the customer.

When you say you'd like to do something, it can also put the customer on alert. It says, "I'm going to ask you to do something," and when customers hear this, they start to resist your persuasion. Substitute these phrases, which preempt resistance: "What we're doing is ..." or "What we'll do is ... ."

41. SOME CUSTOMERS GET A BIG THRILL OUT OF HAGGLING AND NEGOTIATING, BUT I'M TURNED OFF BY IT. WHAT CAN I DO?

Get used to the fact that haggling is here to stay. There are some folks who hail from cultures where it is unacceptable *not* to negotiate! When you're dealing with such a person, it pays off if you start higher, then whittle your prices down to lower levels, based on customer requirements. If you start too low, you'll have no margins to cut.

I don't enjoy haggling either. But it is a fact of life in business, so if you refuse to play the game, you'll be the loser.

42. I Don't Want to Make Cold Calls. Do They Really Work?

Many new and experienced telemarketers dread cold-calling. But the purpose of cold calls is to bring your existence to the immediate attention of folks in your marketing universe. And they may simply not find out about you otherwise.

There are alternatives to cold-calling, but they're expensive, and they're not guaranteed to bring business your way. You could advertise, for instance, and hope that your ads will elicit inbound phone calls or visits to your store, office, or showroom.

One-shot ads seldom do the job, so it takes saturation advertising. This is continuous exposure before a target audience. It isn't cheap, as they say.

Another alternative to the cold call is the use of publicity or public relations. This route is less direct than advertising and much less reliable.

Some firms will try to generate "leads" from direct mailers, trade shows, and other sources. But again, this is costly, and the quality of the lead is always questionable.

So, this discussion has just come back, full circle, to cold-calling.

It's actually a very good way to start your sales career. Here's why:

- The only thing that's harder on a person than cold-calling is failing. Once you have surmounted the cold-calling challenge, your self-confidence will soar.

- If you can successfully cold-call, I guarantee, you'll always make a living. Strong statement, right? Perhaps, but it's true.

  When you cold-call, you take control of your income. You realize that it's just you, your telephone, and the world. And if you're determined, you'll win.

  Cold-calling works because there is always enough business that is unclaimed by your competitors to provide you with a good living. It's like fruit that's hanging off the higher branches of trees.

If you have the motivation to climb up and get it, you'll be able to harvest quite a bit. If you wait until it falls to the ground, it may already be rotten and not be enough to sustain you.

- If you do enough cold-calling at the beginning of your career, you may not have to make another such contact after you become established. This is how it works for many people who sell insurance.

They may have to hustle for the first three to five years, but after that, renewals, referrals, and policy additions by the existing client base can be enough to ensure a sizable number of sales.

So cold-calling creates a nifty income annuity for these salespeople. Cold calls get a bad rap, but they build character and cash flow. Don't fear them; *make them.*

43. How Can I Tell Whether a Prospect Is Worth My Time?

This is almost impossible to know unless you're psychic or at least very intuitive.

When it comes to cultivating prospects, we could all take a tip from the Kenny Rogers song, "The Gambler." He sang: "You've got to know when to hold 'em; know when to fold 'em; know when to walk away; and know when to run."

I heard that the difference between a good manager and a great one boils down to a matter of judgment. When you choose sales as your career, you also choose to manage yourself and your time. And you want to make sure that you exercise good judgment in doing so. Figuring out exactly which prospects are most likely to buy requires the sort of discernment that usually comes with great experience.

Let me give you a perspective on judging the value of your prospects. Some are cherries, and others are pits.

What do I mean? You'll find that cherries are the prospects that are ready, willing, and able to buy. They're what are called qualified leads. Often, they're guarded from salespeople by electric fences, armed guards, secretaries and assistants, and voice mail.

But they're worth pursuing.

Pits, on the other hand, may be infinitely more accessible. They're friendly, happy to chat with you and waste time, and they're almost always available. But they can't, or won't, buy.

Most novices at selling spend time "pit polishing." This involves wasting effort tending to pits in the hope that they'll turn into cherries.

The best thing you can do with pits is dispose of them.

44. How Can I Find a Prospect's "Hot Button"?

It pays to find and to push the customer's hot button, which is the single most important thing that a buyer is looking for. Find it, satisfy it, and you have done your job. It's just that straightforward.

If you're selling real estate, you'll find most buyers are looking for a convenient location, good schools, curb appeal, a nice kitchen, a yard, or a certain number of bedrooms.

Ask prospects to rank their preferences. What won't they live without? What are the "musts"? Play to these priorities and you'll prosper.

45. What's a Good Way to Break the Ice with Customers?

Ask prospects to tell you their professional stories. How did they get to where they are today? Not only will they light up and enjoy sharing these details with you, but they'll probably reveal how they see the business and discuss their values with you. This is the stuff of good relationships. And it's a comfortable environment to create to make prospects feel good about buying from you.

46. As a Manager, Should I Insist Reps Make or Take a Certain Number of Phone Calls?

I'd try to avoid falling into what I call "the quality vs. quantity trap." Many of us have heard that it's preferable to create a limited number of quality results instead of producing a quantity of inferior results.

Teachers say it this way: Haste makes waste.

In certain settings, they are quite right. But in selling, I think you'll find that quantity leads to quality.

Here's how. The more presentations you do, the better you'll get. It's like hitting baseballs in batting practice. You sharpen your batting eye by swinging at more balls. Many of the best hitters are the ones who force themselves to take extra batting practice.

If you swing at too few pitches, you won't be nearly as loose or successful. Some trainers say that the three rules of real estate may be "Location, location, and location." If so, the three rules of success in sales are, "Talk to the people; talk to the people; and talk to the people." Quantity works, and there's nothing wrong with getting that message across to your troops.

47. Can I Get Secretaries on My Side So They'll Willingly Put Me Through to Their Bosses?

One of the biggest frustrations in trying to sell to senior executives is the fact that they are "buffered" from the outside world. They may have legions of assistants whose purpose may seem to be preventing you from reaching anyone.

Don't let them daunt you. Shape your strategy accordingly. Devise a "script" or a set of procedures that will appeal to the proxies.

If you know, for example, that a secretary answers a chief executive's line, don't try to blast your way through to the boss. Instead, speak to the secretary, explain your goal and its benefits to the CEO, and then offer the screener several ways of pursuing a relationship.

You can offer to phone the CEO "by appointment," at a specific time, and actually put it on your respective calendars. Or you can offer to fax or mail information or even have the secretary call you back to suggest the next step.

This may seem like a slow process, but I think you'll find it is the quickest way to get through to buffered buyers.

48. PROSPECTS HAVEN'T HEARD ABOUT MY COMPANY BEFORE I CALL. HOW CAN I ESTABLISH MY CREDIBILITY WITH THEM?

Whenever you can, stake out the "high ground" for your product or service. Make it the front-runner in the prospect's mind. If it wasn't the first on the market, you can still make hay out of the fact that your firm is an up-and-coming organization and a future leader.

Try to position your products as the most advanced and the most useful. In other words, try to find one key distinction that your product can own, all by itself.

What this can do is set up a standard of comparison in the buyer's mind. When he or she comparison shops, the customer will check to see whether others offer your key feature or benefit. If not, you win!

49. HOW CAN I STAY ORGANIZED WHEN I DO MY TELEMARKETING?

Use sales software to keep track of your customers — their interests, purchases, and comments. It may be the best way I have ever found of getting and staying organized. Call your local dealer for names of software that might work for you. But be aware of the fact that using software can usher in certain problems.

When you think of a salesperson, what characteristics come to mind? Glib, personable, and enthusiastic are a few adjectives that might fit.

What about organized? Not really. Salespeople aren't generally high on the idea of filling in a lot of paper work, dotting the *I*'s and crossing the *T*'s. They tend to be big-picture, instead of detail-oriented, people. When they joined the working world they didn't labor over the question, "Do I go into book-keeping or into sales?"

It is their lack of organizational prowess that makes them attractive candidates for lead-tracking software. This product helps salespeople and tele-marketers to capture basic information about prospects and then to set up certain re-call dates for staying in touch with the customers.

It can be handy and effective. But it can easily sidetrack salespeople into wasting their time and energy with prospects who aren't worth pursuing.

Here's what I mean. Let's say you are given a new software package. The first thing you do is load it with a lot of "suspects," or people who you think are worth contacting. The number may easily run into the thousands, if only because this is the denomination through which database vendors sell their lists.

So you have a good PC and thousands of people to call. You start your calls, and inevitably, the great majority result in "No's," in stalls, and in changed names and phone numbers. Naturally, you're going to want to input this information into your new database.

This takes lots of clerical time — time that you could be investing in other calls. One of the painful insights you may have is that you're gilding a wilt-ed lily. If you merely had a suspect to begin with, why go to such lengths doc-umenting changes in its status? Isn't this a supreme waste of time?

Here's a related problem. You contact someone who requests literature. You misinterpret this as an expression of deep interest. You mail it. You enter this information into the database. Three or four days later, you call the person. You get voice mail or learn she's away from the office. Your database asks you when you want to call again? You input the next day.

Same result; so what's next? If you're like most people, you'll feel you have a great investment in the person, as you scan your electronically preserved history with the account.

You won't want to throw in the towel and delete the person from your database because you've been oversold on the value of finding and keeping prospect names. So you add them to your mailing list and repeat the same procedure, to no avail.

As I mentioned earlier, there are two kinds of prospects: cherries and pits. Cherries have a lot of promise, and telemarketers should be looking for them when they prospect. Pits aren't cherries. They consume your time and prevent you from finding cherries.

The problem with lead-tracking software is it discourages sellers from calling a pit, a pit. It implores sellers to treat pits as they would cherries. And this is a tremendously wasteful endeavor.

Tracking every last detail about people who don't matter isn't a virtue. Telemarketers shouldn't allow a machine to intrude on the process of judging the value of various suspects and prospects. Good telemarketers have a gut feeling for when prospects are worth pursuing.

Telemarketers also appreciate that many prospects aren't worth an additional second of their time, and they rightfully jettison the pits into oblivion. Therefore, I recommend that you use sales software, but make sure it's your servant and not your master.

50. How Can My Department Make Phone Calls Seem Much More Personable?

Keep plenty of business cards on hand, put your photo on them, and send them out to the people you contact. They're really the cheapest little billboards that you can find.

One of Monsanto's divisions brought its field sales force inside, and one of the cleverest things managers did was personalize their letterhead with reps' pictures.

By the way, I wouldn't get too creative in designing your stationery, unless you're a graphic artist. The basic "tombstone" look, possibly with a tasteful logo, is the most credible-looking letterhead and business card format to prospects.

51. Is "Networking" Included in Today's Concept of Telemarketing?

Definitely. The basic idea of networking is that everyone knows someone who needs or uses what you sell. You're only four phone calls away from finding anyone in the world!

Ask your clients, friends, and especially your own vendors and suppliers who they know who "uses or might have a need for" what you're selling.

Of course, get their phone numbers and give them a call, mentioning who referred them to you. If they aren't the final buyer you're looking for, they could very well know who is. Then, of course, pursue that lead.

After writing one of my books, I phoned some of the editors at magazines that publish my writing. I left messages on voice mail, mentioning that my book was complete and asking whether any knew of some good agents to represent me.

One fellow called back and left the name of his book publisher. I called him, and he referred me to a person in his company who acquires books in that genre.

I didn't get exactly what I asked for, but I made great progress toward my goal of getting the book into the hands of the right publisher.

By the way, after I mentioned to the publisher the name of the person who had referred me, he said, "Well, I know your name, and our friend would never send me anyone who wasn't first rate."

What a nice reception, right? That's what you can generate when you put network-telemarketing to use.

52. ARE THE BEST TELEMARKETERS ALWAYS SELLING, NO MATTER WHERE THEY ARE?

I think so. I tend to have a definite "front stage" when I have my sales hat on; and a "back stage" when I don't want to open my mouth. But many of the best telemarketers aren't like me, in this respect: They sell *everyone*.

What do I mean? They're high-energy people who figure that they never know when they're going to run into someone who is in the market for what they're selling. So they never completely take off their sales hats.

Let me give you an example of what can happen if you relax too much. I had just finished serving as a consultant to a company. It had been a lucrative, very positive experience for all concerned.

About two weeks later, I sat next to a fellow on a plane who was the senior V.P. of a firm in the same industry. He had heard of my work, and he handed me his business card, asking me to call him.

I recall acting nonchalantly. I really didn't want to talk business, and I wasn't in a mood to discuss the contract that I had completed. Frankly, I felt like I was off duty, and I just wanted to be left alone.

For that moment of solace, I paid dearly. If I had been smart, I would have put on my sales hat and sold the fellow some services, then and there. I'm serious!

You can always relax later.

53. CAN YOU TELL HOW SMART A PROSPECT IS FROM HOW HE COMMUNICATES OVER THE PHONE?

Not at all! Never tell yourself, for instance, that "slow talkers" aren't as smart as faster communicators. Some clients need time to chew on ideas and to thoroughly think them through. If you rush the clients or jump to the conclusion that they aren't comprehending you, you'll often be wrong.

54. IF I'M TRYING TO SELL BIG-TICKET ITEMS TO COMPANIES, SHOULD I START BY CALLING MIDDLE MANAGERS?

I wouldn't. I'd start at the top, by calling senior V.P.s and higher executives, such as presidents. Middle managers are generally too busy, too scared, and too cautious to promote your cause.

Senior executives will have to approve the purchase, so sooner or later they'll need to be involved. Make it sooner, and they'll send you down the line to speak to the right managers in the firm. You'll save time going top-down, instead of middle-up.

55. WHICH SALES GIMMICKS SEEM TO WORK WELL OVER THE PHONE?

Urgency works. People often buy faster when they think time is of the essence. A telemarketer can create urgency by referring to several things.

You can say that there is special pricing, a limited quantity, or an opportunity of some sort that will vanish before too long. Of course, these need to be honest statements. Sellers don't want to lie.

You may feel that resorting to urgency should be unnecessary. I agree. But I'd be denying two realities: (1) Urgency promotes faster and therefore cheaper buying decisions, and (2) it works.

56. I Feel That I'm Interrupting People When I Call. Is That Normal?

Try to remember this at all times: Customers should welcome your calls because you exist to solve their problems and to satisfy their needs.

Therefore, be proud of what you're doing! And please, don't act as if you believe your phone call or visit is an interruption of more important activities. Your contact is extremely important.

Let me give you an example of what *not* to do. Many sellers have been taught to begin a conversation this way: "Hello, Ms. Jones. I'm Gary Goodman with Goodman Communications. Is this a good time to talk?"

Or, they'll ask: "Am I interrupting anything?"

I enjoy answering the office phones because I get to hear how other people are telemarketing. It's not the state of the art that I hear most of the time, but rather, the state of actual practice. And I'm amazed that some bad habits are still being propagated by trainers.

One of the *worst* telephone habits is getting a prospect on the line and immediately asking: "Do you have a minute to talk?"

Whenever I hear this question, I cringe. It asks a prospect to buy a pig in a poke — something he or she can't see. At the beginning of a call, a prospect has no way of evaluating the promise of your conversation, so asking him or her to make a commitment to listen before even knowing you or your purpose is absurd.

I can't imagine saying, "Sure, I have nothing but time to listen to sales pitches!" I don't, and to imply that I have nothing better to do doesn't do too much for my self-esteem.

From the seller's point of view, asking for a minute or two turns on an egg timer, at best. Who wants a prospect who is counting the seconds until the seller is finished?

Often, those kindly prospects who agree to listen hate themselves immediately afterward for consenting to they-know-not-what. You can hear them
giving disgruntled feedback as they listen.

I have always operated on the assumption that people who answer their
phones are saying that they are available, at least for a minute. To ask them
explicitly is, in a sense, redundant. Moreover, it invites a negative response
while actually wasting everybody's time.

Just get to the heart of your presentation. Tell the person why you're calling. If he or she is interested, you will have truly earned a listener and perhaps a sale.

Conversely, if customers don't have time for you, they'll say so soon
enough. Then it's a simple matter of abandoning your effort, or setting a "telephone appointment," through which you can actually reserve their time.

As you know, I've developed a new telemarketing technique that I call the
Perfect Question. It encourages a prospect to buy into a conversation very
quickly or to comfortably disqualify himself or herself from the need to be
communicated with any further.

Given the fact that most people are crunched for time, telemarketers
should sell as if they have time in their calls for only one good question. Let's
make it a winner.

57. Should I Always Take a Customer's Objection at Face Value?

Sometimes objections don't mean what you think. Let me give you an
example. I conduct public seminars. I also publish audiocassette seminars for
those who attend and want reinforcement of the ideas, as well as for people
who couldn't get to the programs.

After I have concluded a seminar tour, I'll inevitably receive calls asking,
"When's the next time you'll be in New York?" or some other city.

If I don't have a seminar scheduled, I'll suggest the audio seminar. My theory is that people are seeking the content primarily, so the medium through
which they receive it is secondary.

Not so, at least for some people. I asked a manager who wished to send two salespeople to a San Francisco seminar why the tapes wouldn't be as effective. After all, he'd save a lot of money in buying them.

He said, to my astonishment, "With the live seminar I'll know my people have attended." In other words, he didn't believe his people could be trusted to listen to the audio program!

About two days later, I had a similar conversation with a former manager, and he said the same thing! I had been assuming that people preferred one medium over another because of performance or convenience factors, and I was completely wrong!

So, look for the objection *behind* the objection, and you'll learn something new.

58. DO HEADSETS IMPROVE TELEMARKETING PERFORMANCE?

They work very well for the people who like them.

The problem I've found is that 50 percent of the reps I've worked with don't like them at all, and so their headsets end up being tossed into desk drawers.

If you're running a high-volume phone center that cues up calls automatically, you'll probably want to make headsets mandatory, because every second counts in that kind of environment, and headsets save time.

On the other hand, if you are part of a small unit or your calls are more leisurely in character, you may want to try out a few pairs of headsets before you invest in them for everyone.

59. IS THERE A CONNECTION BETWEEN MUSICAL ABILITY AND TELEMARKETING ABILITY?

I haven't done a formal study of the connection, but there certainly seems to be a strong link between telemarketing capability and musical aptitude.

Musical ability enables telemarketers to listen for vocal nuances that non-musical folks can't hear. Therefore, singers and others can make sensitive and successful telephone communicators.

60. SHOULD TELEMARKETING MANAGERS ALSO PERFORM SELLING DUTIES?

It can be useful for managers to return to the phones, at least periodically. You may become so accomplished in selling that your company recruits you into management. This happened to me, and it was great.

But it can be a mixed blessing. You can lose touch with the climate in which your salespeople are operating unless you force yourself to put your sales hat back on and hit the phones or the road. I suggest you schedule yourself for selling duties every so often to stay in touch with customer needs and market conditions. It'll also help you to relate to your salespeople.

61. SHOULD WE MAKE OUR CALLBACKS TO CUSTOMERS AT THE EXACT TIME THEY HAVE REQUESTED?

No. When a prospect asks you to call in three weeks, try calling just a little earlier. This will compress the sales cycle and earn you more sales in less time. But you'll also be able to detect whether a competitor has horned in on your action.

When I was in the auto leasing business, a prospect for two Cadillac Eldorados asked me to check back with him in three weeks. I waited until that time. When we spoke, he said: "You're too late! I just leased two Eldos from a dealer."

I vowed to never let that happen again. If you're early, it's usually not a problem. You're just showing a desire to do business.

62. IS THERE A SUREFIRE WAY TO DISTINGUISH "TIRE-KICKERS" FROM REALLY QUALIFIED PROSPECTS?

I wish there were. All I can urge you to do is refrain from judging the value of a prospect by vocal or physical "appearances." In the leasing business, I had an instructive experience that taught me to avoid stereotyping people based on age.

One day, a young man and woman strode into my office. He said he wanted to lease a Ferrari for his girlfriend. I thought they were probably unaware of the cost, so I told them. He didn't flinch, but he did seem impatient.

I took a credit application from him and told him to call me back at the end of the day. I figured he'd never have the credit worthiness to get the car.

Within two hours, my credit manager scurried into my office in an obviously excited condition. This wasn't characteristic of him. He asked me where the customers were, and I said they left. He said: "Lease him anything he wants. He has a trust fund that's worth millions!"

The buyer didn't call me back. Later, I found out that he got his car elsewhere.

63. HOW CAN YOU KEEP ALL THE DETAILS ABOUT TELEMARKETING IN YOUR MIND AS YOU DO IT?

You can't. If you try to treat telemarketing as a totally rational, linear task, you'll trip yourself up with complications. Let me put it to you this way: If you have a choice between thinking and acting, take action.

I think telemarketing is like a sport. You need to learn certain rules of the game and develop your techniques. And you can also learn some refinements from "veterans" like me.

But the real action is on the playing field. You'll learn more by playing the sport than you ever will by thinking about it, talking about it, or analyzing it.

The great educator, Thomas Dewey, said: "We learn everything by doing." So, go get 'em!

64. WHEN CAN TELEMARKETING REPLACE FIELD SELLING?

Telephone chauvinists have always believed that telemarketers could replace field salespeople. Now with corporate downsizing affecting everyone, including traditional sales organizations, the question that is being asked isn't *whether* salespeople can be replaced, but instead, *when* and *how*?

I wrote the best-selling book entitled, *You Can Sell Anything By Telephone!* Whether it's situationally feasible to substitute telemarketing for field selling is another matter. Sometimes customers will accept a "phone-clone" instead of a warm body. Other times, they won't.

Let's examine two case studies drawn from my experience as a telemarketing consultant to determine when telemarketing should or shouldn't be used as a replacement for the sales visit.

The president of a home security firm wasn't happy with his sales routine. He had invested heavily in radio and television advertising to develop leads that his telemarketers would follow up. An appointment would be set by telemarketers for field salespeople, who were responsible for closing deals.

The problem with this approach was the fact that it was time consuming and expensive. The president's idea was to replace the field selling function by having his telemarketers close the deals over the phone.

Theoretically, it should have worked. The firm had a certain amount of name recognition in the marketplace. It also had a proprietary technology that enabled it to actually listen in to a home to hear whether a break-in was occurring.

But there were major problems. While we closed some deals entirely by phone, I felt the percentages weren't positive enough to continue the program. Customers seemed bent on "reinventing the old system." They wanted hand-holding. And the phone link wasn't enough.

I call home security a "sensitive-topic" sale. People buy these systems out of fear. When they're afraid, they have a higher need to develop trust in their vendor. A disembodied phone voice wasn't enough to assuage their fears and help them to develop confidence in the system or vendor. As it turned out, the phone was more effectively used in setting solid appointments. So I recommended restoring the old sales program with a few enhancements.

The chief financial officer of a jewelry company came to me after his firm decided to fire 25 out of its 65 field salespeople. Sales costs were outpacing revenues in such a way as to send shivers throughout the organization. It was felt that telemarketing could service smaller accounts that weren't handled economically by field people.

Jewelry has traditionally been sold in person because buyers are usually investing in its physical qualities, which are often visible to the eye but less amenable to description. So, most people would predict failure for a program that tried to telemarket such items.

But our program prospered. We prepacked a number of jewelry items for purchasers, thus bypassing their impulse to pick-and-choose while looking at catalogs. We also used the fax machine to reinforce our presentations and to give buyers a sufficient idea of the physical attributes of the items.

When all was said and done, we were able to outsell the field sales force by using a deft combination of phone-and-fax, or phone-and-mail. Not only did we service existing "marginal" accounts but also opened a lot of new accounts through cold-calling by phone.

So, the 25 departed field salespeople weren't missed by the company or by their past customers. And the company fulfilled its objective of cutting costs while increasing sales.

Whether telemarketing is an adequate replacement for field selling depends on several factors. Careful evaluations should be made before you leap to the conclusion that "the phone always beats the foot."

65. WHAT'S THE IDEAL ROOM TEMPERATURE FOR A PHONE CENTER?

Seventy degrees Fahrenheit. (Aren't precise answers wonderful?) I didn't get this figure from any survey, but from direct observation. Of course, if you leave the climate control gauge in the hands of phone reps, they'll all take turns setting it to their own personal preferences.

I've found that 70 degrees isn't so warm that folks will yawn or fall asleep. And it's not so brisk that they'll be turning blue, either. At 75 degrees, you can lop off an hour and a half of daily productivity. At 79 degrees, don't even bother asking your people to come back from lunch! They won't be worth a darn.

66. WHICH PRODUCTS ARE EASIEST TO SELL OVER THE PHONE?

By far, the easiest products to sell by phone are the ones with which customers are already familiar and that are somewhat standardized.

The yellow, plastic kitchen trash bags that I mentioned earlier in this book come to mind. When I was consulting for a fundraising group, we asked for a contribution and used kitchen bags as a premium. They worked well because most people have the same size of kitchen trash container, so they weren't getting "a pig in a poke."

67. ARE THERE ITEMS THAT AREN'T COST-EFFECTIVELY SOLD BY PHONE?

I've found it difficult to sell "innovations" by phone. For example, one of my clients came to me with a water-purifying device that he hoped to sell by phone. It was a pen-like dispenser that administered a drop of liquid to a glass of water, which then killed a lot of the bacteria.

I advised my client not to try to use telemarketing to move this product. I felt that it changed the way people thought of pure water, which was that it came in bottles or through a filter affixed to a water tap.

Getting telemarketing prospects to buy a health-related innovation, sight unseen, based solely on a telemarketer's persuasion, was just not going to be cost effective.

I'm sure this advice saved my client tens of thousands of dollars.

68. WHAT'S THE EASIEST CUSTOMER COMMITMENT TO ENGINEER BY PHONE?

I think the easiest thing to accomplish by phone is to set an appointment with a prospect, providing you use an excellent script for doing so.

Generally, people enjoy meeting other people, so they're not all that uptight about sparing a few minutes for a meeting. But you have to sound businesslike and make the client feel that there will be a payoff to getting together; otherwise, he or she won't bother.

69. WHERE CAN I FIND GOOD CALLING LISTS?

Your current customers are the best prospects to contact with telemarketing calls, so formulate them into a list. You can also use list brokers, who can be found under the heading, "Mailing Lists," in the Yellow Pages. But I've found there is even a better, free source of lists: the Internet.

Enthusiasts say the World Wide Web is a great economic leveler. Small companies and individuals can compete with the biggies and use their creativity to attract attention as a substitute for spending big bucks through conventional advertising.

Well, there's another way that the Web can help the financially challenged or the just plain thrifty. It is in developing a free marketing database. Lists are in abundant supply if you know where to look and you use a little creativity to leverage different Web sites.

Why go into cyberspace for a list? Getting lists from brokers can be inconvenient and costly, especially if you're telemarketing. When I go through conventional list sources, I usually have to buy a minimum of 5,000 names. That'll set me back $500 – $1,000, and I'll have to wait a week or two for delivery.

I don't need 5,000 files to make an inference about the viability of a category. I may need only dozens or hundreds of names, addresses, and phone numbers that are geographically concentrated or dispersed.

You can currently go to various free Web sites and download as many basic data files as you want within minutes.

Some sites are intended for job seekers. They'll have as many as 100,000 companies in their databases. The Nationjob Network is an example (see: http://www.nationjob.com/).

One of my favorite free database sites is Switchboard, which contains 10 million companies (see: http://switchboard.com/). You can search by company name and by geographical location.

For instance, I wanted to develop a list of high-tech firms, so I entered the partial word, *technolog*. This brought up about a thousand firms with "technology" or "technologies" in their names.

I got the same result with the word *system*. If you want investment companies or mutual funds, try *investment* or *fund*. And if you want to develop a quick list of a stock brokerage's nationwide branches, type in the name, such as Smith Barney or Merrill Lynch.

Within seconds, you'll be rewarded with a list that you can either download directly or copy into a word processing or database application.

One of the benefits of testing lists this way is the fact that it's private. You don't have to bare your soul to a list broker who could be passing on your marketing moves to competitors. Frankly, I prefer to do my systematic failing (list testing) in private.

And there's a time to use conventional list sources. It's after you've done the preliminary work with free database services that are there in the ether, waiting for you to use, night or day.

70. I HAVE TROUBLE STICKING TO A TELEMARKETING SCRIPT. IS THERE SOMETHING WRONG WITH ME?

Not at all. In fact, it may be "only human" to want to deviate from scripts. Clients approach me all the time and ask: "Can you write a telemarketing script for us?"

It *is* one of the services I provide. But the greatest script in the world won't do any good if it isn't used. The sad fact is that a lot of management energy is put into scripting, whereas reps invest as much, if not more, energy in trying to defeat them.

How come? Several theories have been advanced:

- Reps prefer to use their own words.

- Reps are lousy readers, so they sound "canned" when using scripts; therefore, they fail more often with them than without them.

- Reps don't have the self-discipline to use them (i.e., they're wimps).

- Managers don't have the discipline to require reps to use them (i.e., they're bigger wimps).

- Scripts are simply misunderstood. They scare people just as computers did about a decade ago.

As a manager and a consultant, I see a certain amount of validity in each of these notions. But there may be an even more serious reason reps avoid using scripts: biology.

People could have innate resistance to repeating tasks in identical ways, and this predisposition might have great survival value in the long run. If people do things slightly differently with each "go round," it forces us to try new things and to avoid complacency.

Every now and then, a slight change in method will yield a boon to humanity. Penicillin will be discovered by accidentally exploring molds.

John Lilly, the Harvard researcher on whom the movie *Altered States* was based, performed an interesting experiment. He had subjects listen to a tape that emitted a word every 15 seconds for 15 minutes. Listeners were asked to write down the 60 words they heard.

When Lilly examined their lists, he noticed a wide range of words. That was odd, considering the fact that the tape recorders uttered the same word 60 times in a row!

Lilly's insight was that we distort what we hear. We can't resist the temptation to bend, fold, and mutilate unchanging, boring stimuli. He inferred that this penchant for reshaping things has survival value. The mind forces us to stay alert and to impose novelty even where there is none — at least on the surface.

A study at U.C.L.A. paid student volunteers to sit in a sensory-deprived "white room." It was soundproof and purposely dull.

The longer they stayed, the more they earned. Several subjects reported having hallucinations, and they emerged feeling quite disturbed and disoriented.

"Being paid to do nothing" wasn't fun at all. Again, where there is boredom, the mind creates novelty. And this could very well be a biological imperative.

So, the answer to "Why do I find it hard to stick to a script?" or "Why won't my reps stick to their scripts?" may be more profound than we have thought.

71. How Much Attention Should I Pay to My Inactive Accounts?

A ton! They can be a rich source of new business.

For example, simply by calling past clients two or three times a year, you can accomplish the following:

- You can find out *how they're using your products or services.* I call past participants about my public seminars and I ask them how they're using the information they learned. I discover what was most useful to them over the long term. This enables me to adjust my course content to emphasize the more valued lessons.

- By staying in touch, I can *discover their unmet needs*. If I have a product that can fulfill those needs, I'm able to make another sale. For example, a number of seminar attendees wanted a little more help with implementing my ideas, but they didn't need consulting. I recommended my audio seminars, which ended up being a perfect fit.

- You can find out *who is no longer around*. It's fascinating to see which people change companies. Often, there are patterns.

    Turnover in high-tech companies is much more rampant than in family-owned distribution firms. As a marketer, if one of my goals is to build longlasting relationships, then I would target the latter instead of the former.

- You can *correct your misperceptions*. I thought one manager was less than elated with a seminar that she attended. I called her, did a thorough debriefing, and found that she actually appreciated the program. Two months later, when I scheduled another seminar, she sent four of her associates!

- You can *earn testimonials*. This is an extremely important, yet uncultivated, area for most sales- and businesspeople. It's always valuable to have a positive reference on hand for a new prospect to call or refer to.

    Last year, I was called by someone in the concrete business who had read one of my books. We got to talking about my programs, and he expressed interest in buying one, but he doubted whether he could get approval from his boss.

    "How persuasive would it be if your boss saw a positive letter about me from the Prestressed Concrete Association?" I asked. I faxed it over, and within 24 hours my prospect obtained the necessary approval.

    I called someone who I had trained at Xerox 10 years before. He had moved on to build a great career in the securities industry. I asked him how my training compared to other sources. He said, "Altogether, I've had about nine months of sales training, when you add it all up, and by far, yours was the best!"

He said I could quote him, and I have, with positive effect.

- You can earn referrals. People know other people who can buy. Do what insurance salespeople have been doing for nearly a century — ask for referrals.

But to earn the right to a referral, you should stay in touch with your customers over the long term. Call your client base two or three times a year, and you'll see what I mean. There's gold waiting for you, in your inactive accounts!

72. IF I'M IN NO MOOD TO SELL, SHOULD I STAY OFF THE PHONE?

Not necessarily. It could be a great time to do your telemarketing.

Everyone knows that it's easy to sell when you're feeling good — say, right after you've won the lottery. Now, that's a great time to have role-distance to what you're doing.

Who cares whether people buy? If they do or don't, it's not going to have an economic impact on you, right?

So, you can be as loose as a goose and not give a hoot (or a honk). That's usually the time when you land the *big one*.

Your devil-may-care attitude is mistaken for true confidence in yourself and your product, so people nearly fall over themselves to give you their business.

The same logic applies to feeling terrible. Most of us think that it's awful to feel awful, if you have a day of selling in front of you. Not true. You might do a spectacular job when you're feeling awful because it can't get much worse, can it? You're starting your day in the pits, so the only way to go is up.

One concern may be that sellers will do more harm than good. So what? Plow forward anyway! Yes, you'll sound less than fluent. Who cares? At worst, this will be a private embarrassment, shared only with your prospect.

Who knows, the Pratfall Effect may take over. This occurs when we spill something on ourselves, but we're self-deprecating about it. Suddenly, observers see our funkiness, and we endear ourselves to them.

There's good news for those of us who force ourselves to sell when we're feeling low. The minute we sell something, our spirits soar, and we prove a whole constellation of things to ourselves:

- It doesn't matter what mood you start the day with. What counts is the mood you end it with.

- Attitudes don't always come before behavior. Quite often they follow it. You know, it's like Dale Carnegie said, paraphrasing the psychologist William James: "Act enthusiastic and you'll become enthusiastic."

- Millions of people suffer from real problems, like chronic pain. Yes, they're the ones who listen intently to the Advil commercials. Thank God if you're not one of them. Your pain is in your head, Bud, so get the lead out! (If you are one of these sufferers, you're already tough. Now, apply that grit to selling.)

- Selling is a discipline more than a skill. This is why novices in nearly every area of sales outperform veterans when they start their careers. They do things by the numbers and they succeed.

- Many wise people have said that 90 percent of success is a matter of showing up on time. Show up at the selling opportunity. Make yourself go through the motions. Push yourself, if you must.

It's like what one character said to fighter Jake LaMotta in the movie *Raging Bull*. He was trying to convince LaMotta to agree to a fight. He said: "If you lose, you win; and if you win, you win!"

Selling is like that, no matter what mood you're currently in.

73. Telemarketing Would Seem to Be an Ideal, Work-from-Home Job. Is It?

It can work out well, providing you pay attention to what I call "The Five Ds."

- **Delicacy.** Bringing your business home depends on getting the consent and support of your roommates or family. If they don't want you doing your grind in the next bedroom or in the corner of the living room, it won't happen, believe me.

    Why would they be concerned? They care because you'll be straining certain home resources. You might tie up the phone line with your modem for faxing or e-mailing. Package delivery services will be ringing the doorbell at various times. Extra phone lines will be ringing when others want to meditate or listen to music.

- **Distractions.** I have a big dog who loves to protect her yard. If there were a canine Bill of Rights, the right to bark would certainly be the doggy First Amendment. So when I want to make a sales call by phone, she becomes an inside dog.

    You can't eliminate distractions at home, unless you dig a bunker. People know you're there, so they'll want to interact with you, if only because they perceive they can.

- **Discipline.** Some people associate home with pleasure and relaxation. You'll have to overcome that tendency. Force yourself to begin your work, whatever it is, on time. Whether you quit late or not is up to you.

    Most of us work well when we develop and stick to routines. You know the old adage: plan your work, and then work your plan. Dedicate yourself to doing first what you least want to do.

- **Detachment.** At home, you'll often find that you're selling in front of an unintended audience: your family or friends. They'll walk into your space in the middle of an important presentation, and you'll need to concentrate enough to detach yourself from their presence. They'll need to be told, in advance, that when this happens, you're going to ignore them until after your call is over.

Detach yourself, as well, from embarrassment about the fact that they're seeing your backstage activities. That's the price you pay for working in communal, mixed-functioning space.

- **Delights.** Reward yourself with the perks that working from home provides. I live in the foothills, three winding blocks from an amazing park. It's a great break to walk or jog there.

  If you have exercise equipment, take a fitness break. Hop on a bike or a treadmill for 10 or 15 minutes. It'll boost your spirits and do you and your body a lot of good.

  Address the five Ds, and you'll be more productive in telemarketing from home.

74. What Should I Do to Become the Top Telemarketer Where I Work?

What do extremely successful telemarketers do that puts them into the top 10 percent of all producers? I've identified five key practices:

- **They persist until they succeed.** It's one thing to appreciate persistence or to talk about its importance. But true top-tenners keep-on-keeping-on long after their less successful peers have cashed in their chips.

  Example: I read about a top talent agent who had a simple philosophy: "If I can't do business with you, I'll do business with your successor, because there's always a successor!"

  In our world of high employee turnover, you're almost always guaranteed a second shot at a firm's business. Don't make the error of thinking that one bozo speaks for an entire company, now or in the future. Persist until you win!

- **They try to beat their personal best.** Record-setters are the people who push themselves beyond their past achievements. They realize that staying in the top 10 means constant improvement and never allowing yourself to become complacent.

- **They do what failures won't do.** Average telemarketers hate to learn from prospects by whom they've been "burned." They won't recontact the folks who rejected their offers to find out why they failed — because it's painful.

  But that's where tomorrow's accomplishments lay: in today's ashes. Do thorough debriefings of prospects to determine your strengths and weaknesses. You'll be an important step ahead of the weak egos that can't learn from setbacks.

- **They multiply their value through technologies.** Today's salespeople must become masters of all sales technologies: faxes, telemarketing, e-mail, and the Internet. There is a direct correlation between the resistance salespeople express toward emerging technologies and their future significance.

  The professional telemarketer appreciates that he or she must master technologies or be made obsolete by them or by the people who pay the price of mastering them.

- **They don't squander energy on nonbuyers.** We can't know in advance who will buy and who won't. So, a certain amount of energy will be misspent in the normal course of selling. But one thing the pros avoid is wasting time gabbing with other telemarketers, gossiping about prospects or debating the merits of the company's vacation policy.

  Top-tenners appreciate that fellow salespeople can't buy anything from them, so they avoid wasting precious time on them. Emulating these five practices won't instantly catapult you into the top 10. But it can't hurt your progress.

75. SOME OF MY TELEMARKETING REPS ARE SLIPPING IN THEIR SALES RESULTS. HOW CAN I MOTIVATE THEM?

As a manager and a consultant, I know that there is one thing that is a surefire motivator of seasoned sales reps.

It isn't a contest or a new bonus plan. It isn't even time off to play golf. It isn't any of the trophies or cruises that you read about.

They get the lead out when we bring aboard a raw recruit who catches on immediately after graduating from training. When neophytes start selling right away, that's when the pride of veterans comes back into play.

Veterans can't stand the idea that a newcomer can quietly show them up. Something has to be wrong! A rumor circulates that management has secretly brought in "a ringer" who is just posing as a novice. That's it — it's not real.

But soon enough the veterans see that theory is full of holes. The new person might be half their ages or might have taken selling up later in life, after retiring from government service.

Well, how come the recruit is doing so well? Does she simply have the magic touch, or is it a case of beginner's luck?

It's neither. Novices can out-sell experienced reps because: they aren't "experienced enough" to *not* sell.

New people generally follow directions. If you tell them that they can march to the Moon, they'll simply ask to be pointed in that general direction. When you say that they can get five sales a day, they'll believe it and set their sights, accordingly. They spend less time doubting and more time doing.

The first thing they want to develop is a winning routine. Seasoned reps struggle mightily to detach themselves from routines, because they think they're superior to them. After all, they learn more as time passes, so they can work "smart" instead of working "hard," right? Wrong, wrong, wrong.

It's smarter to work harder. Get back to a winning sales routine. Cut out the fluff, and just do the basics. Again.

You'll be a winner, because you'll be a *beginner*!

I hope this "question-and-answer" section has addressed some of your most pressing concerns. I also hope this book has given you the confidence to try telemarketing and telemarketing management.

I've attempted to convey to you "the good, the bad, and the ugly," when it comes to using this vital means of customer contact and persuasion.

Despite its challenges, telemarketing is a great medium that is worth your investment, both personally and professionally. And I hope it is as good to you as it has been to me!

Good luck!

ABOUT THE AUTHOR

Dr. Gary Goodman is an expert in the field of professional telephone use, especially in the customer service and sales areas. He is in great demand as a speaker and motivator, as well as a consultant who can help companies get the most from their telephone sales and service operations. He has previously authored *Reach Out & Sell Someone* and *You Can Sell Anything by Telephone*. He also writes frequently for such publications as *Call Center Magazine*, *Time* (Internet version), *Direct Marketing News*, and *Sales Manager's Journal*. Dr. Goodman heads the Telephone Effectiveness Institute in Glendale, California. Phone: (800) 451-8355.